Introduction by Shirley Dobson

TEACH US TO
P.R.A.Y.

Studies for Children, Youth and Adults
That Will Get Your Whole Church Praying

Gospel Light is an evangelical Christian publisher dedicated to serving the local church. We believe God's vision for Gospel Light is to provide church leaders with biblical, user-friendly materials that will help them evangelize, disciple and minister to children, youth and families.

It is our prayer that this Gospel Light resource will help you discover biblical truth for your own life and help you minister to children, youth and adults. May God richly bless you.

For a free catalog of resources from Gospel Light, you can call your Christian supplier or contact us at 1-800-4-GOSPEL *or* www.gospellight.com.

PUBLISHING STAFF

William T. Greig, Publisher

Dr. Elmer L. Towns, Senior Consulting Publisher

Pam Weston, Editor

Patti Pennington Virtue, Associate Editor

Jeff Kempton, Editorial Assistant

Kyle Duncan, Associate Publisher

Bayard Taylor, M.Div., Senior Editor, Biblical and Theological Issues

Dr. Gary S. Greig, Senior Advisor, Biblical and Theological Issues

Kevin Parks, Cover Designer

Kevin Parks and Debi Thayer, Interior Designers

Rosanne Richardson, Cover Production

Christi Goeser, Contributing Writer

Acknowledgments to and contributions from: **Pastor Ralph Sikes, Annette Brashler-Bourland, Bonnie Cox, Jeremy Jones and James Weidmann**

ISBN 0-8307-2778-7

How to Make Clean Copies from This Book

You may make copies of portions of this book with a clean conscience if:

- you (or someone in your organization) are the original purchaser;
- you are using the copies you make for a noncommercial purpose (such as teaching or promoting your ministry) within your church or organization;
- you follow the instructions provided in this book.

However, it is ILLEGAL for you to make copies if:

- you are using the material to promote, advertise or sell a product or service other than for ministry fund-raising;
- you are using the material in or on a product for sale;
- you or your organization are **not** the original purchaser of this book.

By following these guidelines you help us keep our products affordable.

Thank you,

Gospel Light

Contributors

Michael Ross is editor of *Breakaway,* Focus on the Family's monthly magazine for teen boys. He is a national speaker and the author of several books for youth. Michael and his wife, Tiffany, live in Colorado Springs.

Norm Rutzen is the pastor of Way of Christ Church in Colorado Springs. He has served in the ministry for more than 22 years and often teaches parenting seminars throughout the United States.

Linda Rutzen is a freelance writer and music minister at Way of Christ Church in Colorado Springs. Linda and her husband, Norm, have two sons, Josh and Jesse.

The P.R.A.Y. acronym was developed by **Bill Muir**, Youth for Christ and Creative Youth Resource.

Contents

CHILDREN'S STUDY

YOUTH STUDY

ADULT STUDY

Introduction by Shirley Dobson

Dear Prayer Partner,

Scripture tells us that Jesus "often withdrew to lonely places and prayed" and that He "went out to a mountainside to pray, and spent the night praying to God" (Luke 5:16; 6:12). He even told His disciples a parable "to show them that they should always pray and not give up" (Luke 18:1). Christ demonstrated for us that intercession is central to a personal relationship with our heavenly Father.

As important as this topic is to Christian life, it's surprising that it is rarely taught. In fact, most people have limited knowledge of true and fervent prayer time with the Lord. Adults particularly need to be rooted in the power of prayer, for they are often seen by youth as examples of spiritual maturity in the Church. In addition, there is no substitute for a deep relationship with God. This is something that everyone can have if they are willing to make the effort to learn.

It is this need for instruction that has led the National Day of Prayer Task Force to provide this resource. It is my desire that *Teach Us to P.R.A.Y.* will be a wonderful benefit to your ministry as you communicate the importance of prayer to your congregation. May God bless your efforts!

Sincerely,

**Mrs. James C. (Shirley) Dobson,
Chairman, National Day of
Prayer Task Force**

How to Use This Resource

It's Time to P.R.A.Y.

If my people, who are called by my name, will humble themselves and pray and seek my face and turn from their wicked ways, then will I hear from heaven and will forgive their sin and will heal their land.

2 Chronicles 7:14

Prayer has been important to God's people from the beginning of time. Not only are we commanded to pray (see Philippians 4:6 and 1 Timothy 2:1-3 for examples), but we are guaranteed of God's action in response to our prayers. And as 2 Chronicles clearly states, if we pray, God promises results.

As a pastor, youth worker, Bible study leader or Sunday School teacher, you have the awesome challenge of motivating those in your care to pray daily. This resource can help. *Teach Us to P.R.A.Y.* features six-week lesson plans specifically targeted to all ages: children (ages 6 to 11), youth and adults.

Empowered with a thoroughly taught and well-practiced prayer life, your church will be transformed by the power of God. What's more, teaching prayer to children and youth is an investment in the kingdom of God—and in the future of our nation and world!

Our Heritage of Prayer

Teach Us to P.R.A.Y. is also an ideal resource for preparing your church for the annual National Day of Prayer (NDP)—a vital part of our national heritage.

Since the first call to prayer in 1775 when the First Continental Congress asked the colonies to pray for wisdom in forming a nation, the call to prayer has continued throughout our history,

including President Lincoln's proclamation of a day of "humiliation, fasting and prayer" in 1863. In 1952, a joint resolution by Congress, signed by President Truman, declared an annual national day of prayer. This law, amended in 1988 and signed by President Reagan, permanently established the first Thursday of May as the official National Day of Prayer. Each year, the president signs a proclamation encouraging all Americans to pray on this day.

The National Day of Prayer stands as a call to us today to come humbly before God, seeking His guidance for our leaders and His grace upon us as a people. It signifies that prayer is as important to our nation today as it was during the formation of our country.

Keep the Flame Burning!

There are many exciting ways Christians can observe the National Day of Prayer. Share this list of ideas with your church families.

• Help your children decorate their bikes with red, white and blue streamers, balloons and flags. They can ride their bikes to the local NDP observance, if possible; or have a parade around your neighborhood.

• As a family project, decorate the exterior of your house with red, white and blue streamers, balloons and American flags. Display an NDP poster on your front door; or mount it on cardboard, attach it to a stake and plant it in your front yard. Be prepared to tell anyone who asks why you're proud to observe the National Day of Prayer.

• Fill in an NDP Prayer Guide and give one to an older child to acquaint him or her with the names of local and national elected officials and the offices they hold. Emphasize the vast responsibilities these officials carry and their special need for prayer.

• With your children, create a special prayer calendar that builds up to the National Day of Prayer and continues throughout the year.

• Take a walk around your neighborhood and pray for each home along the way. Invite another neighbor family to join you in your prayer walk.

• Find out if your community is having an NDP observance and organize a special family outing around the event. Parents take the day off from work, children get excused from school, and all attend the event as a family. Enjoy a picnic lunch together at a park or in your own backyard. Invite another family to join in eating an all-American meal that includes hot dogs and apple pie. Spend time praying and searching God's Word for prayer-related passages.

• Tie red, white and blue ribbons to your car antenna beginning sometime in April. Tell those who ask that you are praying for the country, in anticipation of the NDP.

• Make place mats to use during the week prior to the NDP. Children can draw pictures of Bible characters or patriotic themes and use NDP stickers. Write favorite Scripture verses on the place mats to help children memorize the verses. Cover mats with wipeable, clear plastic, so they can be used several times. Share them with friends and other family members.

- Have a family contest and award NDP T-shirts to the children who can:
    1. Locate all 50 states on a blank map.
    2. Name the president, vice president, your representatives and senators.
    3. Identify the original 13 colonies.

THE P.R.A.Y. BRACELET

The P.R.A.Y. bracelet from the National Day of Prayer Task Force is an excellent teaching aid for this curriculum. The bracelet is designed to solidify the practical application of the lesson by keeping the call to prayer "close at hand" (pun intended). The letters on the wristband will serve as a reminder to the wearer to pray throughout the day.

Constructed in a popular weave style, much like the WWJD bracelets, the multicolored design was fashioned specifically to help youth share the gospel. The five colors—black, red, white, gold and green—represent sin, Christ's blood, purification, heaven and new life, respectively.

By wearing a P.R.A.Y. bracelet, your children and youth will be constantly reminded of the powerful message of God's love and salvation. What's more, they'll be motivated to share the good news with their friends. A helpful explanation card is included with each bracelet.

Call (800) 444-8828 for information on group pricing.

Teach Us to P.R.A.Y.
(Kidz 6-11)

Why P.R.A.Y.?

God made it clear *right from the start* that we must use every opportunity we can to brand our children's lives with the distinguishing mark of His Word. Remember Moses' exhortation to the children of Israel in Deuteronomy 6:6-9?

> These commandments that I give you today are to be upon your hearts. Impress them on your children. Talk about them when you sit at home and when you walk along the road, when you lie down and when you get up. Tie them as symbols on your hands and bind them on your foreheads. Write them on the doorframes of your houses and on your gates.

In other words, a brief bedtime prayer and weekly trip to church is not enough to pour the kind of spiritual foundation that children need. Even a quick family devotion may be fine in its place, but it can't do the whole job of teaching the next generation to know and love God. Living our convictions and demonstrating our dependence upon the Lord day in and day out and from morning to night is the key.

Christian adults must consciously model their faith in God and the reality—the necessity—of prayer. We must never miss an opportunity to speak openly of our love for Jesus in front of our children or to refer to our need for His help in any given situation. This is where the first small seeds of spiritual understanding are sown; this is how genuine trust in God begins to grow in the heart of a child. And this is the point of this curriculum: to allow the opportunity for God to reveal Himself and His great love, through the ever-open door of prayer.

So what is *Teach Us to P.R.A.Y. (Kidz 6-11)*? P.R.A.Y is the acronym for a simple prayer pattern—Praise, Repent, Ask and Yield—that emphasizes the importance and joy of prayer to children. Each week of the study focuses on a different aspect of prayer using the Bible, games, stories, songs, skits—and of course, prayer itself. By breaking prayer down into easily recognizable pieces, children can become confident to pray beyond rote and recitation to real communication. As they move through each of the six lessons, even young children will begin to deepen their prayer times by using this simple acronym.

We've designed this study using a race car theme, presenting prayer as an amazing adventure to new and exciting places; and we've also included ideas for adapting the sessions for younger children. Each session has six sections:

- **Grab Your Keys**—An opening game or activity to get kids primed and ready to explore the theme of the session
- **Rev the Engine**—An opening group prayer activity
- **Check the Map**—Interactive Bible teaching with follow-up discussion questions and suggestions
- **Hit the Road**—A skit or story to help kids apply the Bible teaching to their lives
- **Off and Running**—A final activity to help children apply the Bible teaching outside of the classroom
- **Crossing the Finish Line**—A closing time for reflecting on the session's topic through group prayer time

Our desire is not to turn prayer into a formula but to provide children a simple prayer framework. We want to see kids all over the world grow in their understanding of God's rich and endless love for them. Teaching them how to develop a meaningful prayer time at a young age will set kids' courses for a deep, abiding relationship with Jesus as they grow older. Who knows—maybe you'll even add a new zest to *your* time of prayer too!

God bless you as you take His truth to His lambs.

Amazing Prayer Adventure

Driving Verse

"This is the confidence we have in approaching God: that if we ask anything according to his will, he hears us." 1 John 5:14

Driver's Destination

We can talk to Jesus daily, bringing Him praises and requests, and He always hears us.

Fuel for the Drive

John 10:14; 1 John 5:14

Step 1: Grab Your Keys

This step will help students understand that God hears their prayers because He cares about them.

Familiar Voices

Materials Needed: Your Bible, a long piece of newsprint or butcher paper (for a banner), several colorful sheets of construction paper, non-toxic glue, scissors, wide-tip felt pens, a thumbtack, a CD or audiocassette of approximately 10 sounds (the more varied, the better; e.g., a dog, a plane, thunder, etc.—if possible, have the sound of sheep too!) and a CD or audiocassette player.

Preparation: Following the sample below, use the newsprint to make a P.R.A.Y. banner that looks like a racetrack. Make a copy of the race car on page 24, color it with the pens and cut it out to move along the racetrack each week to illustrate which letter of the acronym the session is focusing on. Place the banner at the front of the meeting room where students will be able to see it throughout the study.

Suggestion: Use clear, self-stick laminating sheets to seal the surface of the banner and race car—this will give you a head start when you go through this study again with a new group of kids! You'll be able to use transparent tape to attach the car at each point on the track without ripping either the car or the banner.

Greet students and begin: **Today we are going to begin an amazing prayer adventure!** Point out the P.R.A.Y. banner and tack (or tape) the race car to the starting line as you explain: **Along the way, we are going to make some wonderful discoveries about God and His love for each one of us. In fact, I'll bet that by the time we're through, you'll be able to tell me at least one thing about prayer that you didn't know before. Are you ready? Good!**

Transition: **The first thing I'm going to have you do is close your eyes.** Explain: **I'm going to play a sound, and I want you to raise your hand when you think you recognize where the sound comes from.** Play the CD, pausing between each sound to give students a chance to raise their hands. When most of the students have raised their hands after a sound, have them call out what they think the source of the sound is. Go through all the sounds (ending with the sheep if you have it); then have everyone open their eyes.

Little People Hint: For younger children, be sure to choose sounds that they will recognize. Also be prepared to repeat a sound if it is unfamiliar to the majority of the students.

Congratulate students on guessing the sounds; then discuss the following questions:

Which sounds were easiest to recognize? The ones that were familiar; the ones that students heard most often.

Which ones were hardest? The unfamiliar ones; the ones that students didn't hear often.

Continue: **The Bible talks about Jesus as our shepherd. What does a shepherd do? Yes, a shepherd is someone who takes care of sheep. A good shepherd takes care of his sheep as if they were his children and he knows them *so* well that he can recognize each one of their voices—even when they're all making noises at the same time! This is because the shepherd loves the sheep and wants to take good care of them.** Read John 10:14; then continue: **Jesus said that He knows His sheep. That means that He knows all the people who belong to God's family—even you and me—and He recognizes our voices!**

Discuss:

What does it mean to pray? Prayer is talking to God.

How do we know that God hears us when we pray? The Bible tells us that Jesus loves us and takes good care of us; He's our very own shepherd. So when we pray, we can be confident that He really does hear our prayers.

When we don't get what we want, does that mean He isn't listening or that He doesn't care? No. God always listens to us, and He always cares about what we need and want. Sometimes, though, the things we want aren't what's best for us and only God can know that for sure. These are the times that He must tell us no—but it's always because He loves us so much that He will only give us what's best for us.

Step 2: Rev the Engine

This step will teach students about one type of prayer—the responsive prayer.

Teach Us to Pray!

Make the transition to this step by explaining: **There are lots of different ways to pray, and we will spend some time talking about them as we make this amazing prayer journey. Right now, we're going to pray a responsive prayer as a group. A responsive prayer is when a leader says a short prayer and the group answers with a one-sentence prayer. This kind of prayer helps us get all our prayers gathered together in one big request; we all are asking God for the same thing at the same time. It's important to think about the response as you say it, because you aren't just saying the words; you're really talking to God! For this responsive prayer, each time you hear me say "Oh, Lord," I want you to respond together by saying "Teach us to pray."**

Little People Hint: For younger children, practice the response once or twice before actually leading them in prayer.

RESPONSIVE PRAYER: TEACH US TO PRAY!

Leader: **Heavenly Father, You know each boy and girl in this room and want each of them to know You, as well. Oh, Lord . . .**

All: Teach us to pray!

Leader: **You want us to learn from Your Word and talk to You every day. Oh, Lord . . .**

All: Teach us to pray!

Leader: **Heavenly Father, we love You and want to grow in our faith. Oh, Lord . . .**

All: Teach us to pray!

Leader: **Amen.**

Step 3: Check the Map

This step helps students realize that God always has time for them.

Never Too Busy

Materials Needed: Your Bible, poster board, a large piece of cardboard, a wide-tip black felt pen, 12 small white balloons, a utility knife, a CD or audiocassette of harp music (or anything "heavenly" sounding), a blank audiocassette and recorder.

Preparation: Write out 1 John 5:14 on the poster board; then create a one-dimensional telephone using the cardboard and utility knife. Use the utility knife to cut out squares for the dial pad numbers; then blow up the balloons (not too full); gently insert them through the backs of the holes to create a Touch-Tone dial pad; then number the balloons similar to the dial pad on a real phone.

Further Preparation: All on one audiocassette, create three different recordings (allow for 10 seconds or so of "dead air" time between each recording) *in order* as follows:

- **Recording One:** *Sound of telephone busy signal.*
- **Recording Two:** *Sound of phone ringing and then harp music. Music fades to voice.* "Hello, you've reached heaven and the office of the almighty, one and only, heavenly Father Himself. Please stay on the line; your prayer is very important to Him. Your call will be answered in the order received. Estimated waiting time: 73,248 million seconds. Have a nice day." *Cut back to harp music.*
- **Recording Three:** *Sound of phone ringing and then harp music. Music fades to voice.* "Hi, you've reached God. I can't take your prayer right now, but don't hang up. At the sound of the harps, please leave your name, age, phone number, shoe size, eye color and favorite food. I'll get back to you

as soon as I can. Remember, there's no request too big or too small for Me. Talk to you soon. Good-bye!" *Cut back to harp music*

Begin by asking for a show of hands:

How many of you like to talk on the phone?

How many of you have tried to call someone but heard this sound instead? Play the busy signal.

What does this sound mean? That the person you are trying to call is already talking to someone else.

Explain: **I need to make an important phone call right now and I was hoping two of you could help me out.** Choose two volunteers who are willing to make a special phone call. Invite them to come forward to your cardboard telephone and explain: **Since we've been talking about prayer and how prayer is simply talking with God, I thought we'd call heaven and see if we can get Jesus on the phone.** (Dig around in your pockets.) **I know I had His number here somewhere.** (Check in your Bible, under a chair, etc.) **Oh wait—I remember it! God's phone number is 777-7777.** After the first student has dialed, play Recording Two.

When the message ends, continue: **That's strange. The operators in heaven put you on hold. Well, let's have our next volunteer try. I'm sure we'll get through this time. Let's try a different number. How about 333-3333?** After the student has dialed, play Recording Three.

When the message ends, discuss:

Can you really talk to God by using the telephone? Be sure to explain that these calls weren't real and that no one can reach God by telephone; this is just a way to get everyone thinking about prayer and talking to God. We don't have to use a phone to talk to God. He is everywhere, so we can talk to Him any*time*, any*place*.

Think about the busy signal. With so many people on Earth, does God ever have to put us on hold when we pray? No. God can listen to everyone who talks to Him, no matter when or where or how many are talking. Explain: **It's one of the amazing things about God. We may not understand how, but we know that He can listen to all of us at one time—and does! Best of all, He always has time for *you*!**

Have students read in unison the driving verse from the poster board (younger students can listen as you read); then continue: **Prayer is a very important part of knowing Jesus. It's how we learn more about who He is and what He wants for our lives. Every day you spend time talking with the ones you love—like your family and friends. Jesus wants us to spend time talking with Him too. This Bible verse tells us that when we talk to God, He always hears us. Even when we don't feel like He's listening—He is.**

Little People Hint: For younger students, be sure to explain the process of telephoning someone, including busy signals and answering machines. One way to do this is to ask them if they have ever made a call, how they did it, what happened, etc. Always start Bible lessons with a familiar, concrete and, if possible, tangible illustration. Never assume anything!

Step 4: Hit the Road

This step shows students that Jesus wants our prayers to be sincere and unselfish.

Talking and Sharing

Materials Needed: A chair, large piece of gold fabric, a paper crown, a book, a cone-shaped princess hat and a cardboard sword.

Preparation: Drape the fabric over the chair to create a throne and place it where everyone will be able to see it.

Begin: **There are two things that will help us when we are praying. I will say them and then you repeat them after me: Pray from your heart. Pray for others as much as you pray for yourself.** Have students repeat the two statements after you three or four times.

Continue: **What do these two statements mean? Let's talk about praying from your heart first. An important part of talking with God is really** *thinking* **about what we're saying. God doesn't want us to say things just because we've heard other people say them. He wants us to talk to Him from our heart about the things that are important to us.**

Secondly, our prayers should not be selfish. This means that we should always ask God for not only our needs but also for other people's needs.

Explain: **Listen as I tell you a story that shows us what we just talked about— praying from our heart and praying for others' needs as well as our own. I will be calling up volunteers to act out the story as I share it.**

> **Little People Hint:** For younger children, it would be better to tell the story rather than read it word for word. This allows your eyes to be on the students and will enable you to better focus on communicating the story. These ideas can be hard for little ones to understand. Keep things at their level by adapting vocabulary and slowing down the pace as needed. Asking comprehension questions as you go will help you know if they are tracking with you or not. If something is unclear, stop and explain it again until the students understand what you're saying.

Choose one of the students to be the king. Place the paper crown on his head; hand him the book; and have him sit on the chair as you narrate the story:

> **Once upon a time, in a land far away, a great and mighty king sat in his royal chamber, reading. He was a very busy king and had a lot of things to do. There was an endless line of important people to greet, laws to make and an evil sorcerer to banish. Glancing up from his book, he looked at the large doors that opened to his kingdom and smiled. Yes, there was a lot to do, but first some people from his kingdom were stopping by for a private visit.**

The first visitor was a beautiful princess. (*Choose a student to play the princess and place the princess hat on her head.*) She walked slowly to the king's throne and curtsied low to the ground. The king smiled and greeted the young lady by holding out his hand to her. But she turned away from him, knelt down and began to pray (*say the prayer as fast as you can*), "Now I lay me down to sleep, I pray the Lord my soul to keep. Let your love guard me through the night and wake me with your morning light. God is great, God is good, let us thank Him for our food. Old MacDonald had a farm. Oops! Amen."

The king was slightly shocked, because even though the princess was talking to him, she was just saying rhymes that weren't really coming from her heart. The king tried to get her attention and said, "Wait! I want to talk with you. I want to hear what's really on your mind, not just fancy words." But the princess didn't take time to hear the king and quickly said, "Forget about the Old MacDonald part. Thanks and good-bye." She got up and quickly left. The king sighed.

The next visitor was a knight. (*Choose a student to play the knight and hand the paper sword to him.*) The knight marched into the king's throne room and shouted, "Your royal highness, there's this amazingly powerful sword I saw while riding through Sherwood Forest the other day. I really want to have it. I need a new sword really badly. I mean, all the other knights will think I'm really important if I have that powerful sword. Know what I mean?"

The king, clearing his throat politely, answered, "It's OK to ask me for things for yourself, but have you ever thought about asking for other people to have the things they need too? Being unselfish really—" The knight interrupted the king, "And another thing! I misplaced my horse. I can't be a real knight without a horse. You find it for me, OK? Well, later." The knight left. The king sighed, again.

While the king was thinking, a young boy entered the throne room shyly, his eyes wide open in awe at the powerful king. (*Choose a small student to play the boy.*) He asked, "Are you *really* the king?"

The king sat up in his chair and smiled warmly, "Why yes, I really am." He offered the boy his hand. The boy climbed onto the king's lap, folded his arms and just waited patiently. The king watched, amazed as the boy sat politely for several seconds. Finally, the king said, "I'm glad you're here. Tell me what is important to you right now."

The boy thought for a moment and then said, "Well, I guess there is one thing I wanted to tell you."

The king spoke, "Go ahead—tell me what's on your heart. What is important to you right now?

The boy answered, "Thank you for inviting me to come here. I love you! That's all."

This made the king very happy and the king and the boy sat there for a very long time just smiling at each other.

Draw out the meaning of the story by discussing:

How are we sometimes like the princess and the knight in the story? Sometimes we forget to pray from our hearts and for the needs of others.

In what ways should we be more like the boy when we pray? We need to remember that God is really interested in what we have to say. We can talk to Him just as we would talk to our best friends.

Why does God care so much about our prayers? Because He loves us and wants to hear all the things that are important to us.

Conclude: **God is our Creator, the King of the whole universe. He is good and loves His people very much. Just as we heard in the story, He listens to each of us whenever we pray to Him—any time of the day, anywhere. When you're scared or sad, God wants you to pray. When you're excited and happy, God wants you to pray at those times too. He wants you to talk to Him about** *everything*!

Step 5: Off and Running

This step helps students learn to memorize Bible verses.

Always Listening

Materials Needed: Several Bibles for students who didn't bring theirs.

 Hint: Keep Bibles on hand that are formatted for kids. It will help them to view the Bible as the great Book that it is, rather than an overwhelmingly too-hard-to-read, I-could-never-finish-this book!

Explain: **We've talked a lot about prayer today. Who can tell me one thing we've said so far?** Let students respond, but guide their answers to include: God hears their prayers because He cares about them; God always has time for them; Jesus wants their prayers to be sincere and unselfish.

Continue: **God loves and hears us when we pray. We can talk to Him anytime about anything that's important to us. Let's read our Bible verse together one more time.** Have students read (or listen as you read) 1 John 5:14.

To help students memorize the verse, play a game of Telephone: Have everyone sit on the floor and form a circle. Whisper the verse into a student's ear. Have that student whisper it to the person sitting next to him or her, and so on, until it goes around the circle. Play the game a few times, starting at different points in the circle to make sure that everyone has a chance to say it correctly at least once.

 Little People Hint: For younger children, use a shortened version of 1 John 5:14 for Telephone.

As you approach the last step for this opening session, consider challenging students to practice five minutes of prayer every day. Encourage them to have their daily prayer time at a certain time each day. The idea is to help them establish the habit of spending time alone with God, giving Him their undivided attention.

Step 6: Crossing the Finish Line

This step will help students grasp the idea of responsive prayer and give them a chance to practice again.

Give Thanks

Explain: **Let's close with another responsive prayer.** You might need to remind students what a responsive prayer is. In this prayer, their response is "Thanks, God!"

RESPONSIVE PRAYER: THANKS, GOD!

Leader: Heavenly Father, You created this world, and You created each person in this room.

All: Thanks, God!

Leader: You made each of us special and unique.

All: Thanks, God!

Leader: You love us so much, You sent Your Son, Jesus, to die on the cross for our sins.

All: Thanks, God!

Leader: Amen.

24

P Stands for PRAISE

Driving Verse

"Praise the Lord because he is so good; sing to his wonderful name." Psalm 135:3 (*TLB*)

Driver's Destination

Praising God not only shows our love for Him—it's also a lot of fun!

Fuel for the Drive

Psalms 47:1; 89:1; 95:6; 98:4; 108:1; 135:3; 141:2; 149:3; John 21:1-4

This step shows students that God wants them to celebrate life.

Celebrate

Materials Needed: All the trimmings for a great party—hats, streamers, confetti, helium-filled balloons tied with colorful strings, a large cake (or cupcakes for everyone), cups, drinks, one birthday candle for each student, matches, candy prizes, a can of *non-flammable* Silly String, masking tape, a CD or audiocassette with festive music, a CD or audiocassette player, a table, one chair for each student and enough room to play a fast-paced game. Whew!

Preparation: Use the decorations to create a party atmosphere in your meeting room. Set the table where it won't get bumped during the highly energetic opening game. Place the cake (or cupcakes), complete with candles, on the center of the table. Set up for a game of musical chairs by placing the chairs back-to-back in two rows. Use the masking tape to mark a safety zone off to the side of the room.

Begin: **Welcome to our second week of P.R.A.Y. Kidz! I'm so glad you're here today.** Take an obvious long look around the room and prompt students by asking: **What do you think we're going to do here today?** Have a party.

Why do people have parties? To honor someone or celebrate their achievements.

What types of celebrations have you been to? Birthdays, weddings, Christmas, graduations, etc.

Little People Hint: Keep in mind that younger children's party experiences are probably limited. You might ask them to share about their last birthday party. Have them describe their cake, the friends and family who came, the games they played and how they felt about being honored at a party. This will make it easy for them to transition to the idea of how God feels when we celebrate Him in praise.

Transition: **Did you know that God loves to celebrate too? It's true! Long ago, when He first led His people out of slavery in Egypt, God gave them instructions about special holidays and celebrations. These special celebrations were to help His people remember the wonderful things He had done for them. Today we celebrate who God is and what He did for us too!** Pass out the party hats, throw some confetti all around and continue: **I hope you're excited about Jesus, because we're going to have a great time of celebration! We've got cake, we've got balloons, we've got drinks, we've got games, we've got surprises—but most importantly, we have a Guest of honor who is smiling with joy over us right now. His name is Jesus, and today we're celebrating the wonderful life we have with Him!**

Count how many students are in the group and remove or add any extra chairs as needed. Invite students to sit in the chairs and explain: **Right now we're going to play musical chairs. When you hear the music start, you need to get up and walk around the** chairs. **Keep walking around until I stop the music; then grab the chair closest to you and sit down. The person who can't find a chair to sit in is out and has to run over to the safety zone** (point it out) **before I can squirt him or her with Silly String!** (Don't squirt students at close range and avoid aiming at their heads.) Start the music and begin the game. While students are walking around, remove one chair from the game. After each round, remove another chair until there is only one chair and two students left. The winner is the student who sits on the last remaining chair.

Little People Note: For younger children, skip the Silly String and do not remove a chair after each round. Instead, let the one who did not find a seat help you with the music until a new student gets out. Young children enjoy participating more than winning, and they will not like having to sit and watch everyone else have all the fun.

Calm everyone down enough to remove all the Silly String (even though it says it's nonflammable, don't take any chances) and have students gather around the cake table. Light each candle as you explain: **As I said earlier, today we're celebrating Jesus and His amazing love for each of us. At a birthday party, we put candles on the cake to show how old the birthday person is. But the candles on this cake remind us of the wonderful life Jesus has given to each of you. There is one candle for each student here. Before we cut the cake, I want to take a minute to talk to God in our hearts and thank Him for the life He has given to us. Let's thank Him for loving us so much.**

Say a short prayer of thanks; then close by blowing out the candles together; then serve the sugar!

Step 2: Rev the Engine

This step draws students back to the focus of the session—praise and prayer!

Back on Track

After regrouping from the party, ask: **Who remembers what a responsive prayer is?** Allow for responses; then sum up: **A responsive prayer is when a leader says a short prayer and the group responds with a one-sentence prayer. This helps us to pray together one giant prayer to God.**

Have everyone join hands and form a large circle; then lead students in the following responsive prayer. Explain: **Each time you hear me say "We call on You, Lord," I want you to say "Teach us to worship."**

RESPONSIVE PRAYER: TEACH US TO WORSHIP

Leader: **Heavenly Father, we want to praise You right now with all our hearts. We call on You, Lord.**

All: **Teach us to worship!**

Leader: **We are glad that You saved us from sin and gave us eternal life! We call on You, Lord.**

All:	Teach us to worship!
Leader:	**Jesus, You deserve all our praise. We call on You, Lord.**
All:	Teach us to worship!
Leader:	**Amen.**

Step 3: Check the Map

The step shows students that God loves to hear their praises.

The P.R.A.Y. Rhyme

Materials Needed: Your Bible, a copy of "Time to P.R.A.Y.!" (p. 32), poster board and tape or nontoxic glue. **Note:** If your photocopy machine can enlarge copies, create the largest copy you can get.

Preparation: Tape or glue the P.R.A.Y. rhyme to the poster board and hang the board where students can see it (leave it there for the rest of this study).

Begin: **Last week we started an amazing journey to better understand how to pray. I want to start today by teaching you a simple prayer pattern rhyme; then each week we will talk about one part of the prayer pattern. Each line of the pattern starts with one of the letters from the word "pray." When you remember the prayer pattern rhyme, you will be able to spend more time talking with God and enjoying it! So here goes—are you ready?**

Point to the "Time to P.R.A.Y.!" poster and ask students to read it together (younger children who can't read can just repeat the lines after you). Repeat the rhyme several times; the goal is to have students become familiar with the whole rhyme, but today you will focus on the first line.

> **Note:** Although the rhyme may sound a little corny, children will remember rhymes and songs much better than plain sentences. (Need proof? How many nursery rhymes can *you* still quote?) To make it more palatable for older students, consider setting the words to a rap beat. You might even use a drum machine if you have one. Bottom line—adapt to your age-group's style, but find a way for them to remember what P.R.A.Y stands for.

Move the race car to just under the letter *P* on the P.R.A.Y. banner (see Session One) and explain: **Let's think about the first part of our prayer pattern:** *P* **stands for praise. What does "praise" mean?** Let students answer; then sum up with the idea that praise is telling God how thankful we are for what He has done for us. Continue: **Our prayers should always start off with our thanking God and worshiping Him. This is our chance to tell God how much we love Him and how grateful we are for what He has done for us.**

There are lots of different ways to praise God. In fact, the Bible tells us several different ways! I'll read a verse, and you can show me how that verse tells us to praise God.

Read each verse from the following list slowly two times and help students find the specific expression of praise mentioned. Ask students to demonstrate each way of praising God before you go on to the next verse.

- Psalm 47:1—Clapping
- Psalm 89:1—Singing
- Psalm 95:6—Bowing down/kneeling
- Psalm 98:4—Shouting
- Psalm 108:1—Playing an instrument/making music
- Psalm 141:2—Lifting hands
- Psalm 149:3—Dancing

Continue: **Praising God means thanking Him and telling Him we are glad that He has blessed us. How we choose to show our praise is not the important thing. You can sing or clap or even shout your praises to God. The important thing is that one way or another you need to take time to tell God how much you love Him.**

Step 4: Hit the Road

This step helps students realize the reason we praise God: because He is *so* good to us.

Praise His Name

Materials Needed: A copy of "Miraculous Catch" (p. 33), an oar, a fishing pole, a fake fish (the smaller, the better), a rowboat (OK, OK, it doesn't have to be a *real* rowboat; use your imagination—a large appliance box cut into the shape of a rowboat, maybe?) and a quick-study adult volunteer to play the role of Peter. **Note:** If you decide to use a real rowboat, you'll need a piano dolly or other means of pulling it offstage and an additional adult volunteer to serve as a stagehand and pull the boat!

Preparation: Give a copy of the skit to an adult to allow plenty of time to rehearse.

Note: This skit can be as elaborate as you like. Use cardboard to create "waves," add background, etc. Let your imagination go wild and give your students a lesson to remember!

Begin: **We've talked about ways to praise God; now I want to tell you a story about a man who discovered *why* we praise God. Let's go back in time 2,000 years and take a peek at a true story that happened on the morning after Jesus rose from the tomb. What began as a pretty gloomy day for a smelly ol' fisherman named Peter turned into a rip-roaring celebration!**

Watch with students as the skit is performed; then award lots of applause to the actor and explain: **Peter left that party with a big zap of hope and a greater sense of purpose for his life. The celebration had just begun when Peter decided to follow Jesus—just as it did for you and me when we received God's gift of forgiveness through Jesus Christ. The celebration hasn't stopped today—and never will! We have life to celebrate—eternal life through Jesus.**

Conclude: *P* stands for praise. Prayer should always start with a joyful thank-you for God's greatest gift—salvation.

> **Note:** This would be a great time to give any students who've not yet received Christ the opportunity to do so. Be sensitive to the Holy Spirit and make the most of every opportunity.

Step 5: Off and Running

This step lets students express praise to God through words and art.

Lots to Be Thankful For

Materials Needed: A long piece of butcher paper, several colorful felt-tip pens, masking tape, a CD or audiocassette of children's praise music and a CD or audiocassette player.

Preparation: Tape the butcher paper to a wall at a level where students can easily write on it. Scatter the felt-tip pens on the floor near the paper. Across the top of the banner write in big letters "Praise God for . . ."

Begin: **We just heard about the greatest reason we have to praise God: our salvation through Jesus. Now let's think of other ways we've been blessed by God.** Have students verbalize both the small and big ways God showers our lives with His goodness. For example: beds to sleep in, people who love us, beautiful trees, etc. Point out many things that children might not typically take time to be thankful for.

Explain: **Let's make a praise banner with words and pictures that tell God how much we love Him!** Point out the butcher paper and invite students to use the pens to draw or write what they want to personally praise God for. Play the praise music as students work.

Step 6: Crossing the Finish Line

We Praise You, Lord!

Gather students in a circle for a closing prayer of praise. Explain: **We've talked about the first part of our prayer pattern:** *P* **stands for praise. Let's end our time together with a responsive prayer that praises God. For this prayer, you'll just repeat everything I say when I give the signal!**

WE PRAISE YOU, LORD!

Leader:	**Heavenly Father, You are so good.**
All:	Heavenly Father, You are so good.
Leader:	**I praise You for everything that makes me smile.**
All:	I praise You for everything that makes me smile.

Leader:	**I praise You for happy times with friends and family.**
All:	I praise You for happy times with friends and family.
Leader:	**I praise You for birthday gifts and pets to love.**
All:	I praise You for birthday gifts and pets to love.
Leader:	**I praise You for helping me in good times and in bad.**
All:	I praise You for helping me in good times and in bad.
Leader:	**I praise You for giving me eternal life.**
All:	I praise You for giving me eternal life.
Leader:	**Heavenly Father, help me to never stop praising You.**
All:	Heavenly Father, help me to never stop praising You.
Leader:	**Amen.**

Time to P.R.A.Y.!

P stands for praise—
that's how we begin

R is for repent—
to turn away from our sin

A is for ask—
what we need God provides

Y stands for yield—
God's the boss of our lives!

Miraculous Catch*

The scene opens with Peter sitting in a rowboat holding a fishing pole. He pulls up the line and groans. Attached to the hook is a tiny fish. He yanks it off and throws it back; then he looks at the audience and begins to speak.

Oh, hi—I didn't see you there. I'm so thankful for some company. Especially since the fishing stinks today. (Well, to tell you the truth, fishing always is kind of smelly!) But let me tell you about a time when the fishing was amazing. It was a day I'll never forget!

It happened on what was one of the worst days of my life. That would be the day my friend—the man I called Teacher for so long—was nailed to a cross. After He was gone, I didn't know what to do, so I went back to my boat.

My friends and I were hanging out at the Sea of Tiberias—doing our best to get on with our lives as fishermen. But for some reason we couldn't even do *that* right. All night we fished, and what did we catch? Zip. Not even one scrawny fish!

Suddenly, I looked up from the water and spotted a guy on the shore, waving.

"Friends, don't you have any fish?" He called out to us. The man acted as if he knew us. "No," we answered.

"Throw your net on the right side of the boat and you will find some."

What? Is this guy crazy? I wondered. The last thing I needed was some landlubber trying to tell me how to fish.

But I had to admit, there *was* something strangely familiar about this guy's voice. And when we did as he said, an amazing thing happened. Fish popped up everywhere! We couldn't even haul in the net because the catch was so big!

John, one of the guys in the boat, was the first to recognize the stranger. And as soon as he let me know who the man was, I couldn't hold back. I did a cannonball right into the water—clothes and all—leaving the rest of my friends to fight with the fish.

Sure, I cared about this incredible catch—after all, I'm a fisherman, right? But that man on the shore was no stranger. He was my buddy, my teacher—my Lord! The One I thought was dead was actually alive and calling out to me!

We had a big feast—a wonderful celebration! We sat around the fire and filled ourselves with the best fish I'd ever tasted. We talked and cried and laughed a *lot*.

Hey, a catch of 153 fish would be worth a party any day, but we weren't celebrating that—right then we had greater things to celebrate. My friend was alive! The man who had been nailed to a cross and placed in a dark tomb was standing face to face with me alive and well! He defeated death! Jesus truly was who He claimed to be—the Lord and Savior.

And even though I had denied Him three times earlier, Jesus didn't stop caring about me. Instead, He hugged me. All the bad things I'd done were forgiven, and I was accepted just as I was.

(Pauses. Strokes his chin and gets a big grin on his face; then looks up.) Let me tell you. What started as the worst day of my life became the first day of my eternal life. The whole world had much to celebrate. Our Savior was with us. God was victorious—praise the Lord!

(Dramatic pause.) Great story, eh? Well, I'd better let you go. Besides, I've got some more fishing to do. *(Waves good-bye and begins to row the boat offstage.)*

* From John 21:1-14.

R Stands for REPENT

Driving Verse

"From that time on Jesus began to preach, 'Repent, for the kingdom of heaven is near.'" Matthew 4:17

Driver's Destination

Repentance means turning away from sin and toward God.

Fuel for the Drive

Isaiah 53:5; Matthew 4:17; 6:9-13; Mark 1:15; Romans 3:23; 1 John 1:9

Step 1: Grab Your Keys

This step shows students that sin means missing the mark.

Missing the Mark

Materials Needed: Your Bible, a large piece of white poster board, a wide-tip felt pen (black), three small spray bottles with stream action, three colors of food coloring, masking tape, a chair (one that you can get wet) and a tarp (to protect the flooring if you can't play this game outside).

Little People Hint: For younger children substitute the squirt bottles with a Velcro ball bull's-eye game, available at most toy stores.

Preparation: Use the black marker to create a bull's-eye circle in the center of the poster board and tape the board to the chair. (**Important:** Don't fill in the bull's-eye; you'll be writing in it during the session.) Set the spray bottles on "stream" and fill them with water; then use the food coloring to make three bottles of colored water, each a different color. Lay out the tarp on the floor and use the masking tape to mark a big X on the tarp where students will stand to shoot at the bull's-eye. (Don't make it too easy to hit the bull's-eye, but do make it possible!)

Begin: **Welcome! I'm glad you're here today. We are going to continue our amazing journey to learn more about prayer. Who remembers the prayer pattern rhyme we began to learn during our time together last time?** Point to the P.R.A.Y. poster with the pattern rhyme and ask: **Who remembers what the letter *P* stands for?** *P* stands for praise. **Great job! Let's say the P.R.A.Y. rhyme together.** Repeat the rhyme several times with students repeating after you; then discuss:

Who can tell me some things we can say or do that please God? As students respond, list their ideas inside the bull's-eye (love, honor, share, obey, pray, etc.).

Now tell me some things we say or do that displease God. As students respond, list these ideas outside of the bull's-eye (lie, disobey, steal, be unkind, be selfish).

Why do you think the things inside the circle please God? Because God's goal for us is that we become more and more like Jesus, living lives that are like the words inside the bull's-eye.

Why do you think the words outside the bull's-eye are things that displease God? Because they are the opposite of how God wants us to live. They are not like Jesus at all.

Continue: **Just like the bull's-eye on this target, God has a way He wants us to live our lives—how we talk, how we treat others, even our attitudes. When we follow that plan, we are hitting the bull's-eye. Every time we don't follow God's plan right, it's like missing the bull's-eye, and it is called sin. Amazingly, sin never stops God from loving us—He always loves us. What sin *does*, though, is stop us from enjoying our friendship with God. Let's play a game and see if we can hit the bull's-eye.**

One at a time, have students stand on the X, aim a spray bottle and fire one squirt at the bull's-eye. Rotate the spray bottles by color to make the marks more distinguishable. Shout "sin" each time a student misses; "glory" each time a student hits the bull's-eye. Don't explain your actions yet. Just continue doing this as each student hits or misses.

Discuss:

How did it make you feel each time I called out "sin"? As if they were doing something wrong.

Why do you think I kept saying "sin"? Because they were missing the bull's-eye.

Was what you were doing a sin? No, it was a game.

Was missing the bull's-eye a sin? Not in this game, but in our lives when we fall short of God's bull's-eye, it is.

What exactly is sin? Anytime we act outside of God's perfect plan for our lives we are sinning.

Little People Hint: One of the hardest ideas for children to understand is that sin is not just the action of disobedience itself. It is a heart inclined toward evil through the fall of Adam. Because we have this bent toward sin in our hearts, we do things that are out of line with God's perfect plan—we sin. Jesus provides a way out of sin by giving us a new heart, one that has the ability to love and obey Him. Today students will leave knowing that the only way out of sin is repentance.

Explain: **The word "sin" literally means to miss the mark. This is why I shouted the word when you missed the bull's-eye. God has a perfect plan—a bull's-eye—for all of His children. He wants them to become like Jesus. Anytime we live in a way that isn't God's perfect plan for us—that isn't like Jesus would live—we sin.**

Continue by asking for a show of hands: **How many of you** *always* **behave exactly the way God wants you to? Not one single human being has ever been able to hit the bull's-eye every day and live a perfect life.** Read Romans 3:23 and explain: **Because we were born with sin in our hearts, we** *all* **miss the bull's-eye and fall short of God's plan.**

If that was all God had to say about our sin, we would leave here very sad, wouldn't we? But there *is* **more: even though we didn't hit the bull's-eye by living perfect lives, Jesus did! He lived a completely perfect life, hitting the bull's-eye every day, all the time. And He offers that life to us! Through Jesus Christ, our sins are forgiven. The target has no more sin stains, just Jesus' perfect hit—right in the center of the bull's-eye. When we come to Him, we are forgiven and He helps us to turn away from sin and to become more like Him.**

Conclude: **Today we're going to talk about the second letter in our prayer pattern:** *R. R* **is for repent.** Move the race car to the letter *R* on the P.R.A.Y. banner and explain: **Repentance is the only way out of sin. When we repent, we receive God's forgiveness and help. So repentance should be a part of our prayer time every day.**

Step 2: Rev the Engine

This step will help students learn the Lord's Prayer.

Our Father

Materials Needed: Copies of "The Lord's Prayer" (p. 41).
   Preparation: Bone up on your sign language for the Lord's Prayer!

Gather students in a circle and explain that you're going to teach them a wonderful prayer—one that Jesus taught to His disciples. Distribute "The Lord's Prayer" and practice repeating the verses, helping students learn the signs that go with them. Once it appears that everyone has it down, pray the prayer in unison.

Step 3: Check the Map

This step will help students understand that when they confess their sins, God forgives them.

In a Flash

Materials Needed: Several sheets of flash paper (available at most novelty or magic-trick shops or hobby stores), a pen or pencil, matches and a metal container to safely burn the flash paper.
   Preparation: Practice burning the flash paper—it burns in a flash, you know!

Caution: Do not, under any circumstances, allow students to burn the paper.

Begin: **We started today by talking about the fact that God has a perfect plan for how we live—special ways He wants us to think, talk and behave. What are some of these ways?** Speaking truthfully, loving others, being diligent, etc.
   Write students' answers to the following question on a sheet of flash paper: **What are some of the things we say or do that are not part of God's perfect plan for our lives?** Lying, being unkind and selfish, disobeying parents, etc.
   Explain: **When Jesus came to earth, He made a very important announcement. He said that people needed to repent because God's kingdom was near** (see Matthew 4:17 and Mark 1:15). **What He was trying to show them was that they must turn away from their old way of living—outside of God's perfect plan—so they would be ready for a new way of living, with God as their Boss.**
   Continue: **The word "repent" means to turn the opposite direction. Let's stand and I'll show you what I mean.** Have students stand and face you. **When I say "repent," I want you to turn away from me and face the opposite direction.** (This

may take some practice with younger kids!) Continue: **Good! Now when I say "repent" again, I want you to turn again to face me.** Hopefully you're seeing all their bright, shining faces!

Transition: **Let's look at our prayer pattern again.** *P* **is for praise and** *R* **is for repent. To repent means to turn and go the opposite direction. And this is what Jesus wanted people to do: to turn away from their sin—living outside of God's perfect plan—and to turn toward Him. Repentance means turning away from sin and toward God. When we pray, we should repent of anything that we have said or done that isn't right. This is called confessing our sin, and the Bible says when we confess our sin, God forgives us and washes it away from us** (see 1 John 1:9).

Little People Hint: For younger children, stop often and assess their level of understanding. If they appear to be having trouble understanding what you're talking about, slow down and repeat the concept again. Having children state in their own words what they hear you saying is a good way to find out what they're really hearing. When you talk about sin, the last thing you want children to think is that God is angry with them or doesn't accept and love them, because they "do bad things." Alleviate shame and guilt by reaffirming that it is *because* God loves them that He wanted to give them a way to be forgiven.

Hold up the flash paper so students can see it and continue: **I wrote down our list of things we sometimes say and do that are not right. How can we get rid of these sins? We could crumple them up** (crumple the paper gently), **but they would still be here.** (Open up the paper and try to smooth it out.) **Now it's just all wrinkled. We could hide them in a pocket** (put the paper in your pocket), **but they're still here. We could rip them up into a million pieces, throw them into the ocean, bury them in the dirt—but they would still be here. So how can we get rid of them?** Allow for responses; then explain: **The** *only* **way to get rid of sins is to repent—turn to God—and confess our sins to Him! The Bible says that when we confess our sins, God forgives us completely.** Place the paper into the metal container; then light it. **He doesn't just hide the sins; He totally removes them!**

Only repentance can allow God's forgiveness to take away our sins. We can't hide them, ignore them or take care of them ourselves. We need God's grace, and we receive that grace when we repent. How can God forgive us? Because Jesus took the punishment for our sins upon Himself when He died on the cross (see Isaiah 53:5).

Step 4: Hit the Road

This step helps students see that repenting is the only solution to sin.

Confess and Repent

Share the following story:

> Chad came home from school and threw his backpack on the kitchen table. He plopped down on a chair and let out a long sigh.

What a day! I'm glad to be home. **The smell of chocolate chip cookies filled the air and drifted right into Chad's nose—fresh, warm, chewy, chocolate chip cookies!**

He sat up and began to scan the counter looking for the evidence of what he was smelling. There, tucked way back in the corner of the kitchen, was a huge pile of his mom's famous cookies. *Oh! My favorite!* **Chad jumped up from his chair and as he began to reach for the plate, he saw a note on the counter next to it that read: "Do not eat. For church tonight."**

What!? How could Mom do this to me? How could she make the whole house smell like chocolate chip cookies and expect me to not eat one (or two or three or four!)? **Chad hesitated for a minute. He peeked around to see if anyone was watching.** *I know she always tells me to ask before taking any food, but—just one. She won't miss just one.* **Gently, Chad lifted the plastic wrap covering the plate of cookies and took one. As he bit into the cookie, the chocolate melted in his mouth and he let out a satisfied "Mmm."**

Right at that moment his mom came in the front door. Chad quickly covered the plate again, grabbed his backpack and ran to his room. *Whew! That was close! I'm sure glad I didn't get caught.*

Follow up by discussing:

What did Chad do that was wrong? Disobeyed his mom and took a cookie.

Thinking about what we've talked about today, what should Chad do now? Repent and confess! Tell God and his mom what he did and ask for forgiveness.

Will there be consequences for his sin, even if he's truly sorry? When we repent, we are completely forgiven by God. Being forgiven doesn't change having to face the consequences of what we did, though. Facing consequences for our bad choices helps us to grow and mature so that we learn to make right choices the next time. Chad will probably be disciplined by his mom, but that's not because she doesn't forgive him; it's because she loves him and wants him to learn from his mistakes.

What lessons can Chad learn from his mistakes? To repent and confess is the only way to be forgiven.

Step 5: Off and Running

This step helps students practice repenting by choosing one area where they need to turn around and go the other way!

Little People Hint: Children learn by example and imitation. Spending a few minutes practicing a new concept is a great way not only to reinforce the lesson but also to clear up any misunderstandings.

Begin: **Let's review our P.R.A.Y. rhyme again.** Have students repeat the rhyme a few times. Consider letting two or three volunteers try to say it without any help.

Ask: **Without looking at the poster, who can tell me what *P* stands for?** *P* stands for praise.

Who can tell me what *R* stands for? *R* stands for repent.

What does "repent" mean? To turn away from sin and toward God.

Why do we need to repent? Because we aren't perfect. We all do things that are outside of the bull's-eye—outside of God's perfect plan for our lives.

Is repentance really important? Absolutely! Because when we let sin stay in our lives, it will stop us from really enjoying our friendship with God.

Does God stop loving us when we sin? God never stops loving us no matter what we do. In fact, it's because He loves us that He shows us our sin so that we can repent and be forgiven. That's why Jesus came. He loves us so much that He made a way for us to be forgiven. He took the punishment for our sins on Himself.

Explain: **Let's take a few minutes and talk to God right now. Think for a minute about one thing that you need to repent of.** Remind students that this could be anything from being disrespectful to their parents to telling a lie, etc. Continue: **Have you thought of something? OK, now confess what you're thinking of to God and ask Him for forgiveness. He will forgive you completely. It's that easy! When you are done confessing, thank Him for His wonderful love.**

Step 6: Crossing the Finish Line

This step helps students reinforce the idea of prayer of repentance.

We Confess Our Sins to You

Have students stand in a large circle and explain that for this responsive prayer, they'll be saying "We confess our sins to You" after you say "Lord and Savior"; then lead them through the prayer.

RESPONSIVE PRAYER: WE CONFESS OUR SINS TO YOU

Leader: **Dear Jesus, we know that when we repent of our sins You always forgive us. Lord and Savior, . . .**

All: We confess our sins to You.

Leader: **We are truly sorry for all the things we've said or done that are not part of your perfect plan for our lives. Lord and Savior, . . .**

All: We confess our sins to You.

Leader: **Help us to become more and more like Jesus. Lord and Savior, . . .**

All: We confess our sins to You.

Leader: **Thank You for Your forgiveness. Make us the kinds of boys and girls you want us to be. Amen.**

The Lord's Prayer

Our Father

which art in Heaven,

Hallowed be Thy name.

Thy kingdom come,

Thy will be done,

In earth

as it is in heav'n.

Give us this day

our daily bread,

And forgive us our debts,

as we forgive our debtors.

And lead us not into temptation,

but deliver us from evil

For thine is the kingdom

and the power

and the glory,

For ever and ever,

Amen.

(Our)

(Father)

(Heaven)

(name)

(come)

(will—
pull hands toward
self several times)

(earth—
rotate hand in
circular motion)

(Heaven)

(give)

(bread)

(forgive—
brush palm twice)

(we)

(forgive)

(lead)

(deliver)

(thine)

(power—
move hand from shoulder
to inside elbow)

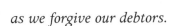
(glory—
clap, then flutter hand in
an arc to vertical position)

(forever)

(Amen)

A Stands for Ask

Driving Verse

"Ask and it will be given to you; seek and you will find; knock and the door will be opened to you. For everyone who asks receives; he who seeks finds; and to him who knocks, the door will be opened." Matthew 7:7,8

Driver's Destination

When we bring our needs to God in prayer, He always provides.

Fuel for the Drive

Psalm 3:5; Isaiah 26:3; Matthew 6:31-33; 7:7,8; Mark 11:24; Ephesians 1:17; Philippians 4:6; 1 Timothy 2:3; 2 Timothy 1:7; Hebrews 11:1; 1 Peter 2:24; 2 Peter 1:3; 1 John 5:14,15

Step 1: Grab Your Keys

This step shows students that God cares about their needs.

Hello? It's Me, God

Materials Needed: A blank audiocassette, an audiocassette recorder, a phone and an adult volunteer.

  Preparation: Prepare for a telephone conversation with God! Record only the phone ringing three times and God's lines from the following script. Pause between each of God's lines in the recording so that you have time to respond. Be sure to practice a few times so that you know exactly how much time you'll need between lines. Here's how the conversation will play out in front of the students:

(The sound of a phone ringing three times.)

You: *(Appear confused.)* Who would be calling right now? Everyone knows we're in session! *(Pick up phone after the third ring.)* Hello?

God: Well hello there! I—

You: *(Look irritated.)* Hi. Hey listen, I have a class I'm teaching right now, so I was wondering it you could call me back later. By the way, who is this?

God: Don't you recognize My voice?

You: *(Open eyes wide.)* Wait a minute. This isn't . . . You aren't . . . I mean is this who I think it is?

God: Yep, it's Me, God.

You: *(Look stunned.)* Wow! *(Talk to students.)* This is my heavenly Father! Can you believe it? *(Back to God.)* Hello, Father! *(Appear nervous and strained.)* I don't know what to say. I'm . . . I'm so glad You called. Is there something You need?

God: Why are you so shocked? I speak to you every day!

You: Yes, but not like this. *(Begin to relax.)* This is great!

God: It's great to talk to you too. Actually, I wanted to talk to you about something that you asked Me yesterday.

You: *(Look worried.)* What? Me ask You for something? Why, I would never do that. I mean I know how busy You are and—

God: No, it was you. I remember and—

Leader: *(Appear flustered).* Of course You do. I wasn't trying to say You didn't remember; but I just, well, I would never ask You for anything, because You are so . . . well, so . . . God! You must have much more important things to think about than my prayer requests.

God: Hey, wait a minute! Your requests are *always* important to Me. I love you very much and I care about the things that are important to you. I called you to tell you that everything will work out fine. I have taken care of it all.

You: *(Appear quiet and thoughtful.)* You mean You are going to answer my prayer?

God: Of course. You asked and I will answer.

You: Really?

God: *(Sound amused.)* Yes, really.

You: Why?

God: Because I love you! Now get back to your class—and tell every one of your students that I love *them* too.

You: Uh . . . OK. I mean . . . thanks! I mean . . . I'll talk to You later! *(Sound of disconnection on other end.)* Wow!

Welcome students and begin: **We are halfway through our amazing journey to learn more about prayer.**

Briefly review the previous sessions:

Who can remember what the letter *P* stands for in our prayer pattern rhyme? *P* stands for praise.

What are some ways that we can praise God? Singing, bowing down, playing an instrument, etc.

What about the letter *R*? *R* stands for repent.

What does repent mean? To turn away from sin and toward God.

Explain: **Great work! This prayer pattern is for you to use when you pray at home. So each day I want you to spend a few minutes talking to God using the prayer pattern we've been learning about.**

Continue: **Today we're going to focus on the letter *A* which stands for ask.** Move the race car on your P.R.A.Y. banner to the letter *A*. Have students repeat "*A* stands for ask" several times. Have students recite the prayer rhyme a few times, mixing up the recitation with individuals, the whole group, boys, girls, students with white socks, students with red shirts or any other creative way you want to practice.

As you are winding up the prayer pattern practice, have the adult volunteer start the audiocassette of the phone call. Answer the phone and have your conversation with God!

After you've hung up the phone, ask for a show of hands: **How many of you talked to God yesterday? How many of you asked Him for something when you prayed?**

Did you know that every time we talk to God He hears us? This phone call was just a pretend call—I wasn't really talking to God. God doesn't need a telephone. He speaks to us in our hearts by His Holy Spirit. I did that pretend call to help you understand that your prayer time is very real. It is just as real as talking on the phone to your mom or your dad or your Great Aunt Gertie. Prayer is even better than talking on the phone, though, because God is listening *all the time*! And He always answers our prayers. Today we're going to talk about asking for things in prayer.

Step 2: Rev the Engine

This step will help students learn how to ask God for the things they need.

Thank You for Giving Us What We Need

Invite students to stand and form a large circle by joining hands. Let them know that you're going to do another responsive prayer and that when you say "Heavenly Father," they are to follow up with "Thank You for giving us all that we need."

Leader: **Lord Jesus, You don't want us to worry about what we will eat or drink today. Heavenly Father, . . .**

All: Thank You for giving us all that we need.

Leader: **You don't want us to be afraid that we won't have the things we need. Heavenly Father, . . .**

All: Thank You for giving us all that we need.

Leader: **Teach us to find our hope and peace in loving and serving You. Heavenly Father, . . .**

All: Thank You for giving us all that we need.

Leader: **Show us how to come to You in prayer for the things that we need. Help us to trust in You. Heavenly Father, . . .**

All: Thank You for giving us all that we need.

Leader: **Amen.**

Step 3: Check the Map

This step teaches students the biblical responsibilities of asking in prayer.

Only His Best

Materials Needed: Your Bible, a "magic" lamp (one shaped like a genie's lamp from a fairy tale), a fan and an electrical outlet.

Begin: **How many of you think that if Jesus said something, it must be true? Of course, Jesus always spoke the truth, because He *is* the truth!** Read Matthew 7:7,8; then discuss:

What did Jesus say would happen when we ask? We will receive.

What about when we seek? We will find.

What about when we knock? The door will be opened.

Explain: **God wants us to ask Him for the things that we need. He is not a stingy God. He is kind and generous and loves to bless His children. Whatever we need, God wants to provide for us as He sees best. Part of prayer is asking, and there are three things we need to know about asking for things in prayer.**

1. Ask in line with God's will—1 John 5:14,15.

Hold up the lamp and explain: **God is not a magic genie who is just hanging around waiting to grant wishes. He is the One true and living God who rules the whole universe by His awesome power. He has given us the *privilege* of coming to Him in prayer, and we are to ask for things that are part of His plan. How do we know what those things are?** Hold up your Bible and explain: **We read about them in His Word. God's plan is in His Word. For example, God has said in His Word that He wants all men to be saved** (see 1 Timothy 2:3). **So we know that we can pray that people will be saved because God has said in His Word that it is a part of His plan. What other things has God said He wants to do? I'm going to read some verses to**

you, and you tell me what they say about God's plan for people. Read the following verses and summarize what they say about God's plan:

Psalm 3:5—Protection and rest

Isaiah 26:3—Peace

Matthew 6:31-33—Physical needs such as food, drink and clothing

Ephesians 1:17—Help in knowing God better

2 Timothy 1:7—A spirit of love, power and self-discipline

1 Peter 2:24—Healing and forgiveness

2 Peter 1:3—Help in becoming more like Jesus

Continue: **Through prayer, we can ask God for anything that is part of His plan for us. What about when we don't know if something is God's plan? Then we ask for God to do what is best and trust Him that He will.**

> **Little People Hint:** For younger children, read the above verses aloud and explain what they say about God's desires for us; then have students act out the ideas. For example, after reading Psalm 3:5, you might explain that God wants them to sleep peacefully and then have them lay their heads down and say "Thank You for peaceful sleep." The important thing is for them to understand that God's plan is revealed in His Word and that they can always pray for what is a part of His plan.

2. Ask in faith—Mark 11:24.

When we ask, Jesus wants us to believe that God hears and answers! This is called asking in faith. Faith means believing something that you can't see (see Hebrews 11:1). Plug in the fan; point it toward the group and turn it on "high." Ask for a show of hands: **How many of you can feel the wind?** Discuss:

Even though you can feel the wind, can you *see* **it?** No.

How do you know it's real if you can't see it? You can feel it.

Explain: **Faith in God is a lot like this wind. We know that because the fan is on, wind is here, even though we can't see it with our eyes. We know that if God has said something, then it is true, whether we can see it with our eyes or not. Faith means believing in what we cannot see. He doesn't want us to be wishy-washy about it. And we can be confident, because we are asking things that we know are a part of God's plan already.** Turn off the fan.

3. Thank Him for the answer—Philippians 4:6.

Explain: **Sometimes God's answers don't come exactly when or how we are thinking they will. This doesn't mean that God hasn't heard our prayers. In those times we must be patient and thankful. God is good and will provide the best for us—even when the best might not be what we thought it would be.**

Read Philippians 4:6 and continue: **Whenever we ask God for something** (demonstrate the sign for prayer) **we need to follow it up with thankfulness** (demonstrate the sign for thanks). **For example, you might ask, "Lord, I need help getting along with my little brother." You can add a second part to that prayer by saying, "Thank You for helping me." We ask** (show the sign and have students imitate it); **we thank** (show the sign and have students imitate it).

Our Father

which art in Heaven,

Hallowed be Thy name.

Thy kingdom come,

Thy will be done,

In earth

as it is in heav'n.

Give us this day

our daily bread,

And forgive us our debts,

as we forgive our debtors.

And lead us not into temptation,

but deliver us from evil

For thine is the kingdom

and the power

and the glory,

For ever and ever,

Amen.

(Our)

(Father)

(Heaven)

(name)

(come)

(will—
pull hands toward
self several times)

(earth—
rotate hand in
circular motion)

(Heaven)

(give)

(bread)

(forgive—
brush palm twice)

(we)

(forgive)

(lead)

(deliver)

(thine)

(power—
move hand from shoulder
to inside elbow)

(glory—
clap, then flutter hand in
an arc to vertical position)

(forever)

(Amen)

Repeat the signs several times to be sure students have learned them; then conclude: **We thank God right away because we know that God hears our prayers and begins to answer them as soon as we ask.**

Step 4: Hit the Road

This step gives students a peek at a Bible character who was thankful for an answer to prayer.

A Very Thankful Man

Materials Needed: An assortment of robes and shawls to use in a skit based on Luke 17:11-19.

Explain: **The Bible tells a wonderful story about a man who did just what we've been talking about** (based on Luke 17:11-19). **He went to Jesus asking for help and told God he was thankful for His answer to prayer. I'm going to need some volunteers to help me tell the story, so listen carefully!** Begin narrating the story, adding volunteers where directed.

One day as Jesus was walking to Jerusalem *(choose a volunteer to play Jesus and give him a robe to wear)*, **He came across 10 sick men** *(choose 10 volunteers to play the lepers and give them robes or shawls to wear)*. **These men had a disease called leprosy. Today if someone has leprosy, doctors can cure the sick person with medicine; but back then, leprosy was not curable. There was no medicine available that would make it go away.**

In order to keep the disease from spreading, people with leprosy were forced to leave their homes and families and live outside of the city by themselves. People with leprosy couldn't even go into the town to visit with friends or family. It was a sad and lonely way to live.

When the 10 men saw Jesus coming, they called out to him, "Lord! Master! Help us!" Jesus didn't run away from them or ignore them. Instead, He turned and looked straight at them. The men asked Jesus to heal them. Jesus felt such love for these men. He didn't want them to be sick. He didn't want them to have to live away from their families and friends. So He told them to go to the temple and show themselves to the priests. The priests were the only ones who could allow a leper back into the city by saying that he or she no longer had leprosy.

When Jesus told them to go, the men knew that He was going to heal them. As they walked along the dusty road to the temple, the leprosy began to go away. Jesus had really healed them! The priests allowed them back into the city—back with their friends and families. They were all well!

One of the 10 men came running back to Jesus and thanked Him. He bowed down and told Jesus how grateful he was for being healed. Jesus placed His hand on the man and asked where the

others were. The man did not know. He was the only one who had come back to thank Jesus. Jesus smiled at the man and told the man to go back home.

Conclude: We should always remember not only to ask God for His will but also to thank Him when we pray.

Step 5: Off and Running

This step gives students an opportunity to make a prayer list and thank God for the answers.

Ask in Faith and Thankfulness

Materials Needed: A report-style folder (with metal brads to hold paper) for each student, copies of "My P.R.A.Y. Journal" (p. 51), notebook paper and pens or pencils.

Preparation: Make prayer notebooks for students by inserting 10 pieces of notebook paper into each folder. **Option:** If you want to get really fancy, make a P.R.A.Y. Kidz label for the front and a title page with the P.R.A.Y. rhyme!

Explain: **Let's take some time now and think of some things that you'd like to ask God for in prayer. You can draw a picture of those things or write words to describe them. Remember, we are asking God for things that are part of His plan; we are asking in faith and we are asking with thankfulness.** Encourage students to ask for the little and big things, assuring them that if something is important to them, it's important to God. Students need to know that their requests matter to God, because He loves them dearly.

Allow several minutes for students to write in their notebooks; then ask volunteers to share one or two of the things they've written or drawn. Consider having the whole group pray with students for their requests.

Little People Hint: For younger students, offer suggestions if they don't know what to do. Things to pray for and be thankful for are keeping their families safe and healthy, watching over their pets, etc.—these all touch on what's important to them. They need to know that if it's important to them, it's important to God.

Step 6: Crossing the Finish Line

Lord, Help Me to Ask

Explain: **Let's end our time with an echo prayer. An echo prayer is simple: you will repeat everything I say when I give you the signal. Are you ready to talk to Jesus?**

Good! Use the following echo prayer to end this session:

Leader: **Lord, help me to never be afraid to ask for help.**
All: Lord, help me to never be afraid to ask for help.
Leader: **Lord, help me to seek You and Your plan for my life.**
All: Lord, help me to seek You and Your plan for my life.
Leader: **Lord, help me to trust that You will provide everything I need.**
All: Lord, help me to trust that You will provide everything I need.
Leader: **Amen.**

My P.R.A.Y. Journal

Y Stands for Yield

Driving Verse

"Submit yourselves, then, to God. Resist the devil, and he will flee from you." James 4:7

Driver's Destination

Part of prayer is yielding our lives to God.

Fuel for the Drive

Psalm 139:16; James 4:7,8

Step 1: Grab Your Keys

This step will help students think about who is in control of their lives.

Who's in Control?

Materials Needed: A remote-control car and several objects to create an obstacle course (e.g., blocks, cans, toys).

Preparation: Set up an obstacle course in a place where students will be able to easily watch the car run the course. Be sure to include some difficult obstacles as well as easy ones. You'll want to keep the volunteers from getting through the course without knocking at least one thing over.

Greet students and ask for a show of hands: **How many of you have used a remote-control car before?** Explain: **I need a volunteer to try to drive my car through this obstacle course without knocking anything over.** Choose a student to come forward and control the car. Instruct the volunteer: **Your job is to guide this car from the start to the finish without bumping into anything.** After the volunteer has gone through the course, reset the obstacles and choose one or two more students to try.

Discuss: **What would happen if I let a baby drive a car on a real racetrack?** The car would crash.

What if a real race-car driver drove around a real racetrack? The car would probably go from start to finish without any trouble.

Transition: **Our lives are a lot like this car. We have a road to travel—our life—and there are many things that get in our way and try to get us off of our course. We need a guide to get us from the start to the finish. God is our guide. When we give control of our lives to Him, He will lead us through our lives and help us avoid any accidents along the way.**

Sum up: **There is a big difference between the car and us, though. The car is like a robot. It goes wherever the signal from the controller tells it to go. We are not robots. We must choose to let God guide our lives and be the One who guides us. We must ask for His help and then obey Him. This is called yielding to God.**

Have students repeat the word "yield" a few times. It's apt to be a new vocabulary word to many! Continue: **For our prayer pattern, yielding means asking God for His guidance and then going in the direction He tells you. How do we do this? We do it through prayer, of course!**

Little People Hint: For younger children, scale down the difficulty of the course and, if possible, let each student have a quick turn trying to drive the car. Young children need hands-on learning to solidify the concept you are introducing. They can understand this analogy if it is presented in simple terms through patient teaching.

Step 2: Rev the Engine

This step will help students ask Jesus to guide their lives.

Take Control of My Life

Have everyone stand and lead students in a responsive prayer. By now they should be very familiar with this type of prayer. Explain: **Let's start today's lesson by praying another responsive prayer. For this one, when you hear me say "Oh, Holy Spirit," you'll say "Take control of my life!" Now let's bow our heads, quiet our hearts and talk to Jesus.**

> *Leader*: **Dear Jesus, we want to be more like You. Oh, Holy Spirit, . . .**
> *All*: Take control of my life!
> *Leader*: **Help us to live in a way that pleases You. Oh, Holy Spirit, . . .**
> *All*: Take control of my life!
> *Leader*: **Let others see You through our words and actions. Oh, Holy Spirit, . . .**
> *All*: Take control of my life!
> *Leader*: **Amen.**

Step 3: Check the Map

This step helps students understand what it means to yield their lives to God.

Give It All to Him

Materials Needed: A copy of *The Living Bible*, a backpack, a pencil box, a baseball, a photo of a family, a jump rope and an apple.

 Preparation: Place all the items in the backpack (you'll be pulling them out one by one during the session).

 Begin: **Today we're going to continue our amazing journey to learn more about prayer. Who remembers the P.R.A.Y. rhyme?** Refresh students' memories and repeat the rhyme several times as a group.

> **Note:** Other review options to consider are letting student volunteers come forward to lead the rhyme, having a contest between the boys and girls or dividing the group into four sections and assigning each section one of the lines to recite. Vary the approach so students don't tune out and just say the words. The idea is to let the words be a *meaningful* reminder of the concepts you have been talking about for the past four weeks.

Congratulate students on remembering the rhyme—and its meaning; then explain: **This week we are going to focus on the last part of the prayer pattern: yielding to God.** Move the race car to the letter *Y* on the P.R.A.Y. banner. **Who can tell me what the word "yield" means?** Allow for responses; then continue: **To yield means to give something up to someone else. When we talk about yielding to God we're talking about giving up our own ways and choices and letting Him be the One leading and guiding our lives.**

Read Psalm 139:16 from *The Living Bible* and explain: **This Bible verse tells us that God had a plan for us even before we were born. He already knew exactly what He wanted for each of us—He had a perfect plan. It's good to yield our lives to God, because He created us and knows what is best for us.**

Transition: **Remember the remote-control car we raced earlier? We said that we were like that car. We need God to guide us, because He knows the course He set for us, so He is the best One to lead us through it. When we pray, we can yield our lives to Him and He will make sure that we stay on track with His plan for our lives.**

Place the backpack where students can see what you'll be taking out. Explain: **What do we need to yield to God? Well, one thing we can yield to Him is our schooling.** Take out the pencil case and hold it up. **We can give our schooltime to God and ask Him to guide and help us learn what we need to learn.** Have students repeat: "Lord, I yield my schooltime to You."

We can yield our sports activities to God. Take out the baseball. **We can ask God to take control of our attitudes so we can be example of good sportsmanship to others.** Have students repeat: "Lord, I yield my sports activities to You."

We can yield our families to God. Take out the photo of a family. **God wants us to serve and honor our families, and we do this with His help and guidance.** Have students repeat: "Lord, I yield my family to You."

We can yield our playtime to God. Take out the jump rope. **We can ask God to guide our playtime and friendships so that they honor Him.** Have students repeat: "Lord, I yield my playtime to You."

We can yield our bodies to God and ask for His help in keeping them healthy. That means we treat our bodies as His house because His Spirit lives in us. Take out the apple. Have students repeat: "Lord, I yield my body to You."

Sum up: **When we yield, we give our lives to God—how we live, how we spend our time, whom we play with—to God's guidance. He is the expert, and we need His help and wisdom.**

The Bible tells us "Submit yourselves, then, to God. . . . Come near to God and he will come near to you" (James 4:7,8). It's up to us to yield to God. And the way we yield to God is by praying and giving control of our lives to Him.

Step 4: Hit the Road

This step shows students that God will guide them to better choices and happier lives if they listen to His instructions.

God Knows Best

Ask for a show of hands: **Who likes to go camping and backpacking? Anyone who has spent any time in the great outdoors knows the dangers you sometimes face—steep cliffs, wild animals and even the hot sun. That's why it's especially important to yield to the leaders and obey their rules when you're outdoors. Listen as I tell you a story about a boy who learned this lesson—the hard way!** Share the following story:

"I don't believe him," Scott told Andy as they packed.

"But he's the guide. He knows what's best," Andy replied.

"Andy, why do we have to take so much drinking water? It makes my backpack too heavy."

"I'm not sure, but Ken's our leader, and he's hiked on this trail a million times. He knows what's best."

Scott and Andy were going on their first backpacking trip. Ken, their guide, had explained earlier that they all would need to take lots of drinking water. "If you don't have enough water to drink, you might get sick."

"Did you bring your sunscreen?" Andy asked.

"Of course," Scott answered. "But only to make my mom happy. Sunscreen's for sissies."

"But—" Andy started.

"But nothing. I've been camping before, and we don't need all this stuff."

Early the next morning, the group took off hiking. The sun rose, and it started to get hot.

"All right, guys," Ken said, "we're going to take a break. Drink some water and put on more sunscreen."

"Here, Scott, you can borrow some of my sunscreen," Andy offered.

"No way, I don't want to smell like bananas all day," Scott said, making ape sounds and accidentally spilling his water.

"Don't be such a jerk. Here, take a drink of my water," Andy said.

"I'm fine. C'mon, let's get going."

The group hiked the rest of the day. They had covered a lot of miles when Ken suggested they stop and make camp.

"The sun is starting to set. After we get the tents up, change into long pants and shirts. Then drink some more water."

"Aren't you thirsty, Scott?" Andy said.

"Yeah, I guess so."

"What's wrong?" Andy asked.

"My arms and legs are sore," Scott said, pulling off his socks.

"You're totally burned!" Andy said, looking at Scott's red legs.

"And it hurts to move. I don't want to change."

Andy went out to help with dinner.

"Where's Scott?" Ken said.

"He's not doing so well. He's still in the tent."

Soon Scott was shivering and needed medical treatment. Ken gathered the group later in the evening. "If Scott had listened to my instructions, he wouldn't be sick right now. When I tell you something, it's for your own good. I'm not kidding around."

Andy thought back to the night before. He had tried explaining to Scott that Ken knew best, but Scott wanted to be in charge. Now the only thing Andy could do was pray for his friend to be healed of his sickness—and his hard-headed thinking.

Discuss:

Why did Ken give all of those orders? Because he was the leader. He had the experience and knowledge to know what was needed for everyone to safely backpack.

Why didn't Scott want to follow Ken's advice? He was stubborn and he thought he knew better.

How would Scott's trip have been different if he had obeyed Ken? He wouldn't have gotten sick; he would've enjoyed the trip more.

Explain: **Just as Ken knew all about backpacking and what was best for Scott and Andy, it's the same way with God. He knows everything and is the best Leader we could ever have! He will guide us to better choices and happier lives if we listen to His instructions.**

God knows best—there's no denying it. His rules are to keep us protected and safe from harm. God's rules are found in His Word—the Bible. When we read the Bible, we need to obey what God has said. When we do, we are yielding to Him and asking Him to guide us through His plan for our lives.

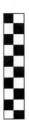

Step 5: Off and Running

Clear Vision

Materials Needed: Six chairs, a blindfold and two pieces of wrapped candy.

Preparation: Set up the chairs as obstacles (a fairly easy course) around the room.

Explain: **Things always go better for us when we yield to God and listen to His instructions.** Ask for two volunteers to illustrate your point. Explain that Volunteer One is going to try to get through an obstacle course with the guidance of Volunteer Two. Blindfold Volunteer One and spin him or her around once or twice; then instruct Volunteer Two to guide Volunteer One through the obstacle course to the end.

Little People Hint: Don't go overboard with the spinning. You don't want any injuries or upset stomachs! A simple turn once or twice is sufficient. For younger children, have the volunteer actually lead the blindfolded student across the room. The idea is the same—God leads us in the best path as we yield to Him.

Instruct students to be quiet so that the blindfolded volunteer can clearly hear the other volunteer's directions. Have them go slowly so that no one gets hurt. This is *not* a race—it's an illustration.

When the students have completed the task, award a piece of candy to each one and explain: **We've talked a lot about yielding to God. In this exercise, Volunteer One represented us—mankind. The guide, Volunteer Two, represented God. God can see everything perfectly clearly; He knows how to avoid every single obstacle that life puts in our way. When we yield to Him, He will guide us to the best choices for our lives. We can trust that His plans are the best plans. And He will walk *with* us to see that we make it all the way to the end.**

Step 6: Crossing the Finish Line

Your Will Be Done

Conclude: **Let's close by praying the Lord's Prayer. When we say "Let Your will be done," we are asking God to control our lives—we are yielding to Him in prayer.** Practice the prayer and hand signals a few times to refresh students' memories; then ask everyone to stand and repeat the prayer and signs in unison to close this session.

Go into the World

Driving Verse

"But the LORD said to me, 'Do not say, "I am only a child." You must go to everyone I send you to and say whatever I command you. Do not be afraid of them, for I am with you and will rescue you,' declares the LORD."
Jeremiah 1:7,8

Driver's Destination

God wants us to make prayer a priority—especially as we share His message with others.

Fuel for the Drive

Jeremiah 1:7,8; Matthew 5:14-16; John 1:4,5,12; 8:12; Romans 3:23; Ephesians 5:8; Hebrews 9:14; 1 Peter 3:18

Step 1: Grab Your Keys

This step helps students see that their faith in God can bring hope to others.

Jesus Lights the Way

Materials Needed: Your Bible, a flashlight for every two to four students, a bag of individually wrapped candies, lunch bags and a large room that can be darkened.

Preparation: Hide the candy in the room for a treasure hunt. (The room will be dark, so don't hide the candy too well!)

Little People Hint: For younger students, be sensitive to the fact that some of them may be afraid of the dark. Provide dim lighting, such as a nightlight or two, for security as well as safety.

Welcome students to the final session of their amazing prayer journey. Begin by reviewing the P.R.A.Y. rhyme. Ask students to call out what each letter stands for; then have the whole group recite the rhyme several times. Encourage students to let their journey continue by daily praying through the P.R.A.Y. pattern they've been learning about.

Begin: **Let's start our last session with a treasure hunt!** Divide the group into teams of two to four students each and give each team a flashlight and a lunch bag. Designate one person in each team as the Keeper of the Light (he or she will hold the flashlight) and the others as the Treasure Hunters (the ones who gather the candy).

Ask: **Who's ready for some tasty treasure hunting?** When all the yelling dies down, explain: **I've hidden some candy in another room, and it's just waiting there for you to find it; but here's the catch: The room is very dark. You'll need the flashlights in order to find the candy.**

Note: Before playing, set clear ground rules such as no running, no screaming, no purposely bumping into each other, etc. (especially for the older students). Make sure everyone understands the behavior expected and the consequences of not obeying the rules—in this case, no more treasure hunting!

Lead students to the room and give them five minutes to find as much candy as they can. After five minutes, give the signal to stop the treasure hunt and lead everyone back to the meeting room. While students are indulging in their treasures, discuss:

How is the dark room like the world around us? The world is dark with sin (see John 1:4,5).

How is a flashlight like Jesus? Jesus brings light and hope into the world (see John 8:12).

Would you have found the candy without the light? No, it was too dark.

Hold up your Bible and explain: **God has given us the biggest flashlight ever—His Word! The Bible tells us everything God wants us to know about how to love Him and how to help others love Him.**

Read Ephesians 5:8 and continue: **We can shine His light anytime we want, any place we want, just by speaking His Word. Prayer helps us to know how to tell others about Jesus and gives us the boldness to do it! So let's continue with our prayer journey, learning how God wants to use us to tell others about Jesus.**

Step 2: Rev the Engine

This step will help students understand that they can ask God to make them bold enough to follow Him.

Lord, Make Us Bold!

Instruct students to stand in a large circle; then lead them in the following responsive prayer. Explain that each time they hear "And so we ask," they should respond "Lord, make us bold to follow You!"

> *Leader:* Lord Jesus, we praise You for the awesome life You've given to us. And so we ask . . .
> *All:* Lord, make us bold to follow You!
> *Leader:* We need Your Word and Your guidance in order to live by Your plans. And so we ask . . .
> *All:* Lord, make us bold to follow You!
> *Leader:* We need Your strength and courage to make good choices. And so we ask . . .
> *All:* Lord, make us bold to follow You!
> *Leader:* Amen.

Step 3: Check the Map

This step shows students that sharing their faith makes the world a brighter, sweeter place.

We Are His Lights

Materials Needed: Your Bible, a flashlight, a box with a lid, milk, three clear plastic cups, three spoons and a bottle of chocolate or strawberry syrup (or have both on hand to give students a choice).

Begin: **We've been talking about how we can bring light to others by sharing God's Word.** Read Matthew 5:14-16 and continue: **Because we know the Light—Jesus Christ—we are the ones who have the job of telling others about Him. Just as I wouldn't turn on the flashlight and then stick it inside a box** (turn on the light and place it inside the box), **I don't want to take the light that comes from God's Word and keep it hidden in my heart only. I want to tell others so they can have His light too. Every time we speak God's Word, it's like turning on a Jesus light** (take the flashlight out of the box) **so that others can see it and come to know Him. When we share His Word, we make the world a brighter, better place.**

Ask for three volunteers who really like milk and give each volunteer a clear plastic cup. Explain: **Let's pretend that this cup of milk is the world around us.** Pour a little milk into each cup; then continue: **Now, I want each of you to take a small sip. How does it taste? Like milk, of course! If you like milk, then it tastes OK. Kind of bland, but good. How about adding some flavoring to liven it up?**

Hold up the bottle of syrup and explain: **Let's pretend that this syrup is telling others about Jesus. Watch what happens when I add it to the milk.** Add the syrup and give each volunteer a spoon to stir the milk and syrup together. While they're stirring, continue: **The whole glass of milk changes color.** Have volunteers take a sip. Ask: **Does it taste any different now?**

Sum up: **Just as the syrup changed the milk, our faith in Jesus changes the world around us. God doesn't want grown-ups to tell others about Jesus, He wants all of His children—including *you*—to spread His message. It doesn't matter to God how old or young you are; He can use you to sweeten the world with His Word.**

Read Jeremiah 1:7,8 and explain: **Jeremiah was a boy when God chose him to tell people about His plan—and not just people but whole countries! At first Jeremiah was afraid. But God told him to speak and Jeremiah did.**

God can use you too, but it isn't always easy. Sometimes it's hard to tell others about Jesus. That's why we need to pray. We can ask God for courage and wisdom to tell others about His Son, Jesus, and He will help us! Jesus also wants us to pray for the people who don't yet know Him. We need to pray that they will listen and understand what it means to make Jesus the Lord of their lives.

Step 4: Hit the Road

This step will give students a chance to make a P.R.A.Y. bracelet that will help them remember the basics of the gospel message.

A Colorful Reminder

Materials Needed: Yarn (or similar product to use for making a bracelet); black, red, white, gold and green plastic beads with openings large enough to thread the twine through; scissors and several adult volunteers.

Preparation: Cut the yarn into 10-inch lengths, one for each student; then tie a knot about two-thirds of the way down each piece.

> **Little People Hint:** For younger children, make sure the beads are an appropriate size to avoid choking. Another option is to have students make keepsake books from the same colors as the beads in the bracelets. Decide what size you want the books to be; then cut strips of black, red, white, gold and green construction paper for each student. Children can put their books together as you explain what each color represents and then you can ask adult volunteers to walk around and staple the books as they're completed.

Begin: **Can anyone here think of someone who doesn't know how much God loves him or her?** Allow for responses; then continue: **All around us are people who need to hear what Jesus did for them. God has given us the job of sharing His Word with those who need to hear it. But sometimes we don't remember what to say or how to say it, so we're going to make a prayer bracelet that will make it easy to tell others about Jesus.**

Have students sit down and give each one a piece of yarn and one bead of each color. Have adult volunteers stationed throughout the room to assist students. Explain: **These colors can help us remember what Jesus did for us, so we can easily tell others.**

Instruct students to thread the black bead on their bracelets and explain: **Black is the first color because it shows us what our lives are like before we give them to Jesus. They are dark and stained with sin. The Bible says that** *everyone* **has sinned; no one is perfect** (see Romans 3:23).

Ask: **What does black remind us of?** The sin in our hearts.

Continue: **Now add the red bead to the twine.** Allow time for everyone to do this while you explain: **Red shows us the only thing that can take away sin—the blood of Jesus** (see 1 Peter 3:18). **Jesus died on the cross for our sins so that our sins could be washed away forever. He did this because He loves people so much that He didn't want to live without them.**

Ask: **What does red remind us of?** The blood of Jesus that washes away all our sin.

Continue: **Next, thread the white bead.** Allow time for students to do this. Check with the adult helpers to be sure everyone is keeping up; then explain: **White shows us what our hearts look like after Jesus washes them—clean and holy** (see Hebrews 9:14). **The blood of Jesus washes away the stain of sin and lights our hearts with friendship with God. Would you rather have a black, sin-stained heart or a clean, holy heart?**

Ask: **What does white remind us of?** A clean and holy heart.

Continue: **Now thread the gold bead.** As students are working, explain: **Gold reminds us of heaven. When we believe in God's Word and receive the gift of forgiveness from Jesus, He promises that we will live forever in heaven with Him.**

Ask: **What does gold remind us of?** Living forever in heaven.

Continue: **The very last bead to thread is the green one.** Have the adults check to make sure students all have their beads in the correct order as you explain: **Green is the color of trees and plants and reminds us of the new life that Jesus gives us when we become part of His family. Belonging to God is the most important thing in life. We can come to know Him through His Son Jesus if we just open our hearts to His forgiveness** (see John 1:12).

Ask: **What does green remind us of?** Our new life in Jesus.

Explain: **OK, let's go through our bracelets together and see if we can remember what the colors stand for. I'll call out the color and you tell me what it reminds us of. Black.** The sin in our hearts. **Red.** The blood of Jesus that washes away all our sin.

White. A clean and holy heart. **Gold.** Living forever in heaven. **Green.** Our new life in Jesus. **Great job!**

Have students repeat the sequence aloud several times until they can get through it reasonably well on their own. Then have students pair up and use their bracelets to tell each other the salvation message. After they've each shared, have them switch and share with new partners. This may seem like a lot of repetition, but children need the repetition to solidify what is taught.

Conclude: **Now you have a special reminder of what Jesus did to make us a part of God's family, and you can tell others! Every time you share God's Word you are shining His light in the darkness, leading other people to the truth.**

Step 5: Off and Running

This step connects prayer to evangelism.

Sowing the Seeds

Materials Needed: Gardening tools (hand shovel, hand rake, watering can, flowerpot, soil and seeds) to use as props during the teaching.

Explain: **Now that we know what to say to others about Jesus, let's look at how prayer is a part of sharing God's Word. Think of a farmer.** (Hold up the shovel.) **He digs up the dirt so he can plant seeds in it.** (Dig; then scatter the seeds in the soil.) **When we pray for people who don't know Jesus yet, we are like that farmer. Only we aren't planting corn or potatoes, we are planting prayer seeds.** (Scatter more seeds.) **God will use those prayer seeds to make hearts ready to accept His Word.** (Water the seeds.) **Every time you pray that God will bless someone, He does. Every time you ask Jesus to help someone, He does. Every time you pray for people to know Jesus, seeds are planted that will someday grow into answered prayer!**

Jesus' whole reason for coming to Earth was to save us from sin, to make the black stain of sin white again. Nothing except His own blood could do it. And He wants everyone to how much He loves them and what He did for them. We can pray that people will understand what Jesus did and accept His gift of forgiveness.

Ask: **Who'd like to plant some prayer seeds? It's easy! Just close your eyes and think of someone who needs to know Jesus or someone who needs to know Him better. Then silently pray for that person. Your prayer could sound something like, "Father, help my friend John to know how much You love him and what Jesus did for him so that he could be forgiven. Amen."** Allow a few minutes for quiet prayer time; then, if you feel your group is ready, have students divide into small groups to pray for the people in your city who are lost—that they would come to salvation through Jesus Christ. Continue to allow them to pray until *they* stop!

> **Note:** Students learn by modeling and imitation, so they need specific examples—especially for abstract ideas like prayer and evangelism. Don't hesitate to lead them in a repeated prayer if they seem stuck. Eventually they'll respond in their own way and wording.

Step 6: Crossing the Finish Line

This step will encourage students to continue their wonderful journey of prayer!

The Journey Never Ends

Materials Needed: Copies (lots) of "Don't Forget to P.R.A.Y." (p. 66).

Explain: **Well, you did it! You made it through our amazing prayer journey. Congratulations! I have great news, though: the journey doesn't stop here—it goes on forever. Now that you have a prayer pattern to help you, you can spend time every day talking to God and growing in your friendship with Him. Let's end our time together by saying our prayer pattern rhyme one more time.** Have students stand and recite the prayer pattern rhyme as a group. Distribute "Don't Forget to P.R.A.Y." and encourage students to use the chart to mark the progress of their daily prayer time.

Close the study by praying a blessing over each one of the students. You might consider having elders or pastors from your church join in blessing this new generation of prayer people, commending them to the faithfulness and grace of God.

Don't Forget to P.R.A.Y.

Use this chart to mark off each step as you P.R.A.Y. every day!

	Sunday	Monday	Tuesday	Wednesday	Thursday	Friday	Saturday
Praise							
Repent							
Ask							
Yield							

Teach Us to P.R.A.Y. (Youth 12-17)

How to P.R.A.Y.

Prayer is powerful. It's not just saying a few words or making a bunch of requests—it's intimate communication with our eternal God. Imagine that! The Creator of the universe welcomes us into His presence. He even delights in it!

Prayer is a gift from the Lord and the work of the Holy Spirit. It's the key to being empowered, as well as a skill we must develop for successful Christian living.

Bottom line: *Prayer is an essential part of every believer's life.*

Yet how many times have you heard a teenager in your care say something like "I don't know how to pray" or "What's the point"?

The fact is too many Christian youth (and adults) neglect prayer. They either don't know what it is or haven't fully grasped the importance of this amazing activity.

We challenge you to turn your youth group upside down for Christ—or is it right side up?! Help them discover the power that comes from an active, on-fire prayer life.

You're holding a six-week curriculum that will get your group started. Using the acronym P.R.A.Y., students will learn the elements of prayer: Praise, Repent, Ask and Yield. Any youth worker can plug this resource into a variety of settings: a Sunday School class, a small-group study, a weekly youth-group meeting, or even a camp or retreat.

THE PLAN

Get Radical!

An introductory session designed to get students pumped up to P.R.A.Y.!

Praise

The first element of P.R.A.Y. is praise. Show students that God is so awesome He deserves our praise.

Repent

The second element of P.R.A.Y. is repent. Teach students about the importance of repentance and seeking God's forgiveness in prayer.

Ask

The third element is ask. Make it clear to students that the Father wants us to share our hearts' desires with Him.

Yield

The final element is yield. Teach students to yield in obedience to our Lord and Savior.

Putting Prayer into Practice

The last session has an evangelistic focus, designed to motivate students to reach out to those who do not have a relationship with Christ.

STEP-BY-STEP

Each session features four sections for creating a fun, interactive learning experience.

Power Up

Begin the session with activities or games with object lessons meant to engage students in the topic, including an opening prayer.

Solid Truth

Interactive Bible studies and discussion starters lead students into God's Word.

Higher Ground

Attention-getting story or skit and a brief talk help students further explore their understanding of God's Word.

Revolution Time

During this, the closing step of each session, students will be challenged weekly to apply the Word to their lives.

Get Radical!

The Message

Prayer is vital to every Christian's life.

Key Verse

"And pray in the Spirit on all occasions with all kinds of prayers and requests." Ephesians 6:18

Biblical Basis

Joshua 1:5; Psalms 5:3; 55:16,17; 61:1,2; Daniel 6:10; Mark 16:15; John 14:13; 16:24; Acts 1:8; Romans 8:26,27; Ephesians 6:18; Philippians 4:6,7; Hebrews 12:18-24; 1 John 4:4; 5:14

Power Up

God cares about our needs and hears our prayers.

Frisbee Frenzy

Materials Needed: Lots of room for tossing Frisbees, one Frisbee for every student, a chair, a long piece of rope (10 feet or so), transparent or masking tape, 3x5-inch index cards, one piece of paper, pens or pencils and one felt-tip pen. **Note:** Defray your supply costs by asking students to bring their own Frisbees for this step. Let students know that you'll have loaners available for those who don't have one to bring. **Optional:** A new Frisbee for the winner.

Preparation: Position the rope in a semicircle around the chair. Use the felt-tip pen and the paper to create a bull's-eye sign with the word "Creator" in the center. Use the tape to fasten the sign to the chair; then place the chair approximately 15 feet from all points on the semicircle.

Distribute index cards and pens or pencils; then ask students to write a one-sentence prayer on their cards. Instruct students to tape the cards to the tops of their Frisbees; then at your signal, everyone is to throw his or her Frisbee at the bull's-eye. Those who hit the bull's-eye with their Frisbees get to stay in the game; everyone else is out.

Move the chair three more feet away from the rope and give the signal for the remaining competitors to throw their Frisbees at the target again. Continue the game until there's only one student left standing; then award the champion with a huge round of applause (and a new Frisbee?). Discuss:

- **Does God ever get confused when He hears our prayers?** No. God is God. Unlike us, *He* can listen to everyone at once. Best of all, He always has time for us.
- **Like all those flying Frisbees, do our prayers ever miss the mark: the Lord's ears?** There are roadblocks to prayer such as unconfessed sin and wrong motives.
- **What should we do if we sense roadblocks in our prayer life?** Pray about it. Confess the sin and repent.
- **Does a person have to be a superjock Christian with a good aim to get his or her prayers through to heaven?** God doesn't care about our physical abilities, our looks or how smart we are. He loves us all just the same and listens to everyone. To be more effective pray-ers, we do need to be in a growing relationship with Him.

Explain: **No doubt about it—there is a lot of confusion spinning around about prayer. And, sadly, the ones who are confused are us.**

Share the following alarming statistics:

- **Nearly 6 billion people inhabit this planet. It's estimated that more than 4.1 billion of them don't know Christ.**
- **Of the nearly 2 billion people who claim to be Christians, fewer than half pray or read their Bibles daily.**
- **While more than 80 percent of North American evangelical Christians say they believe in the authority of the Bible and the power of prayer, more than 50 percent of them also believe that absolute truth does not exist.**

Ask for a show of hands: **Raise your hand if these facts disturb you. Raise your hand if these facts make you want to stand up and do something. Before we go deeper, let's pause for prayer.**

NOTE

We cannot assume that students know what absolute truth is, particularly in the present postmodern culture. But an understanding of absolute truth is essential to acceptance of God's Word and the need for every human to acknowledge and accept Jesus Christ as Savior.

Give your students some concrete examples of what absolute truth is.

- God exists and He created the heavens and the earth.
- Some things are always wrong and some things are always right regardless of the circumstances.
- "All have sinned and fall short of the glory of God" (Romans 3:23).
- "God so loved the world that he gave his one and only Son that whoever believes in him shall not perish but have eternal life" (John 3:16).

Lead students in the following prayer:

Lord, I ask You to help me to see the importance of prayer. Help me to make it as natural as talking to a friend. Help me to see that, through prayer, I am actually talking to the greatest Friend of all—YOU.

Solid Truth

*There is a divine purpose—
and a real need—for prayer.*

Communication

Materials Needed: Several Bibles.

Distribute Bibles and ask a volunteer to read Ephesians 6:18. Discuss:

- **What's the definition of prayer?** Communicating with God.
- **Why is prayer so important to a Christian's walk with Jesus?** Our faith in Jesus Christ is a personal relationship, and communication is important for every relationship. Prayer is our personal communication with God.
- **What are some excuses we tell ourselves for our lack of prayer?** Too busy, pressures of life, etc.
- **What are the real reasons behind our lack of prayer?** Selfishness, sin, etc.

Explain: **In Joshua 1:5 the Lord says, "I will never leave you nor forsake you."** God is the King of the universe, yet He listens to us humans. He has extended His hand to you and invites you to share whatever is on your mind—anytime, any-where. Pause and give students a moment to consider this amazing fact; then continue: **During the next few weeks, we are going to plunge into prayer and learn the meaning of ultimate** *power*, **ultimate** *peace* **and ultimate** *purpose*.

Higher Ground

When we need help, God wants us to call on Him.

Staring Down a Lion

Materials Needed: Several Bibles, copies of "Staring Down a Lion" (p. 76) and "Let's Talk" (p. 77) and pens or pencils. **Note:** If you have an overhead projector, consider cre-ating a transparency copy of "Staring Down a Lion," instead of copying it as a handout.

Distribute "Staring Down a Lion" (or show the overhead) and explain that the Bible tells a story about a man of God who knew a lot about prayer. Ask for several volunteers to take turns reading the handout; then discuss:

*   **What was Daniel's priority in life?** His faith in God and prayer.
*   **How did everyone know Daniel served God?** Through his lifestyle of committing to prayer and yielding to God.
*   **What did God do as a result of Daniel's yielding his life?** God protected him and blessed him.
*   **How would a Daniel-type believer look in today's world?** An ordinary person (like you or me) who is wholly committed to God in word and deed.

Explain: **Radical obedience, unwavering submission to the King of kings—that's how Daniel lived his faith. He didn't know exactly what would happen to him in the pit of the lions' den, but he did know this: God is God, the one and only God—and He can be trusted even when a dozen lions are poised to pounce. And Daniel was committed to prayer.**

Do you talk regularly to your eternal King—God? Really talk *to* **Him, not** *at* **Him? Don't just pray with canned, programmed expressions that sound nice. Dare to be like Daniel. Dare to discover the power of prayer!**

Divide students into small groups of four to six. Distribute "The Power of Prayer" and pens or pencils; then instruct students to use the questions on the handout as a basis for small-group discussion.

Revolution Time

He left it all up to us.

Back to the Truth

Explain: **It's time for a revolution—a spiritual revolution. Today, more than ever, this planet needs a true counterculture. We need a back-to-truth movement. If ever there was a group designed for such a task, it's a group of teens who radically follow Christ—no matter what!**

Before Jesus ascended into heaven, He gave us a big job: "Go into all the world and preach the good news to all creation" (Mark 16:15). He also gave us a bunch of assuring promises, including these three:

1. "Surely I am with you always, to the very end of the age" (Matthew 28:20).
2. "You will receive power when the Holy Spirit comes on you" (Acts 1:8).
3. "The one who is in you is greater than the one who is in the world" (1 John 4:4).

Continue: **How incredible God is! He is the God of the universe—the alpha and the omega, the beginning and the end—yet He forgives our sins, promises us eternal life with Him *and* gives us the power and authority to fulfill His work on Earth. To top it off, He even stays with us every step of the way! OK, where's the catch? Actually, there's not one, other than believing and accepting Christ into our hearts—*but* our work for Him on Earth won't be effective if we don't make prayer a priority over all other things. How do we do that?** Use the following information to explain two major keys to making prayer a priority in our lives.

Key One: Know What Prayer Is—and What It Isn't

Prayer is *not* going through the motions, saying a bunch of thoughtless, mechanical words or phrases (as some people quickly do before a meal). This isn't to say that reciting written prayers with a heart full of praise for God isn't OK—but relying on them as a sole means to talk to God isn't enough.

Prayer *is* communicating with the one and only eternal God. Kenneth Taylor said it so well: "He is the incredible God who created everything there is, and who is in control of the universe, which is expanding at the rate of 186,000 miles a second in all directions every hour. You, as God's child, can come right into His presence where He joyfully welcomes you because you have become His."[1]

Key Two: Stop Making Excuses

Just do it! Amazing as it may seem, Christians of all ages and walks of life make lame excuses for avoiding prayer. "I don't know what to say," "I don't know how to pray!" or "I'm too busy" are common.

If you've figured out how to talk to a friend on the phone or how to send e-mail on the Internet, then you know how to pray. It's simple: Jesus is your best friend and He wants you to tell Him about everything that's going on in your life. He wants to know the desires of your heart, how badly you feel when you fail, how happy you are when good things happen. Even though He already knows everything that happens in our lives, He doesn't want to be a spectator; He wants us to *share* our lives with Him.

Prayer Time

Close the session in prayer, thanking God for His desire to have a one-on-one relationship with each and every one of His children and asking Him to open the lines of communication for those who feel that talking to Him is difficult.

Note
1. Kenneth N. Taylor, *Words and Thoughts to Help You Grow* (New York: Inspirational Press, 1998), n.p.

Staring Down a Lion

Imagine, if you will, traveling to a time long ago to a city named Babylon. You are there to observe a young man named Daniel.

The driving force in Daniel's life is obedience to God. Radical, unwavering submission to the one true King—even at the risk of losing popularity, prestige, position. Even in the face of a totally pagan culture that worshiped many gods, including a sun god, a water god, the god of prosperity, etc. Could you do it? Could *you* stand firm, as Daniel did?

Daniel had seen the Master's hand move in amazing ways—especially the time when three fellow believers were thrown into a blazing furnace for refusing to bow to the golden idol. The flames were so hot in the roaring furnace that King Nebuchadnezzar's soldiers died throwing Shadrach, Meshach and Abednego into the fire. Yet, when the king ordered the furnace reopened, the men of God stepped out unharmed. Not even a single hair on their heads was singed! (See Daniel 3:12-25.)

"Praise be to the God of Shadrach, Meshach and Abednego. . ." Nebuchadnezzar proclaimed. "They trusted in him and defied the king's command and were willing to give up their lives rather than serve or worship any god except their own God" (Daniel 3:28).

Now, many years later, the opposition to God and His people continues. An observer may wonder, *Will the hard-hearted people of this world ever learn?* Babylon's administrators—jealous of Daniel—have convinced the new king, Darius, to issue a crazy decree: "Anyone who prays to any god or man during the next thirty days, except to you, O king, shall be thrown into the lions' den" (Daniel 6:7).

Daniel doesn't flinch. He kneels at his upstairs window—the one opened toward Jerusalem—and prays three times a day, giving thanks to God, just as always.

"Did you not publish a decree . . . ?" the administrators ask the king (Daniel 6:12).

"The decree stands," Darius replies, and Daniel is quickly thrown into the lions' den. "May your God, whom you serve continually, rescue you!" the reluctant king tells Daniel (Daniel 6:16) as a stone is placed over the mouth of the den.

Will Daniel's life end with the fierce swipe of a lion's paw? Not a chance! Just as He did for Shadrach, Meshach and Abednego in the furnace, God protects and prospers His obedient children. To the king's great surprise—and delight—Daniel not only survives his encounter with the lions but also emerges unscratched! Overjoyed, King Darius proclaims, "For he is the living God and he endures forever; his kingdom will not be destroyed, his dominion will never end. He rescues and he saves; he performs signs and wonders in the heavens and on the earth. He has rescued Daniel from the power of the lions" (Daniel 6:26;27).

Let's Talk

The Power of Prayer

Look up the Scripture references to find clues to the answers to the questions.

Romans 8:26,27; Philippians 4:6,7

Define the word "prayer"—what is it and why is it important?

Hebrews 12:18-24

Why does God want us to make prayer a priority?

What are some of the things He wants us to pray about?

Psalms 5:3; 55:16,17; 61:1,2; Ephesians 6:18

When is the right time to pray?

When did David pray?

Was David always happy when he prayed?

1 John 5:14

What does it mean to pray according to God's will?

John 14:13; 16:24

How can you have God's power in *your* life?

Praise

The Message

God is so awesome He deserves our praise.

Key Verses

"Praise the LORD. Praise the name of the LORD; praise him, you servants of the LORD, you who minister in the house of the LORD, in the courts of the house of our God. Praise the LORD, for the LORD is good; sing praise to his name, for that is pleasant." Psalm 135:1-3

Biblical Basis

Psalm 135:1-3; John 14:9-26; 15:9-17; James 4:8; 5:13-16

Power Up

God wants us to celebrate the life He gave to each of us.

Praise Is a Celebration

Materials Needed: A table, party hats, streamers, confetti, lots of Silly String, pizza, cupcakes, drinks, cups, napkins, candy prizes, a video camera, blank videotape, a TV and a VCR.

Preparation: Do your best to create a party atmosphere. Hang streamers on the walls and ceiling; decorate the refreshment table with a colorful tablecloth and confetti.

Also, arrange for a volunteer to walk around during the party, filming 10 minutes or so of students demonstrating their ideas on what it means to praise God. Have the volunteer encourage students to be creative: acting out a spontaneous skit, singing songs, hosting a "talk show," etc.—the sky's the limit!

Welcome students and explain: **Praise helps us to focus on God. We forget about ourselves as we pray and give Him the honor He deserves. And when we praise God, we draw close and acknowledge our dependence on Him. Today we're going to begin with a party—otherwise referred to in the Bible as "praise!"**

Distribute the party hats (don't forget to wear *yours*); bust out the Silly String and host a party!

Celebrate for about 15 minutes; then ask everyone to sit down to watch the praise video *they* just starred in. After the video, lead students through the following prayer:

> **Lord, please teach us to pray. Teach us to commit our hearts to You. Teach us to hear Your voice, to obey Your will and to never stop praising You.**

Solid Truth

God is awesome and deserves our praise.

He Is Worthy

Materials Needed: Several Bibles, copies of "Let's Talk" (p. 82) and pens or pencils.

Distribute Bibles and ask a volunteer to read Psalm 135:1-3. Discuss:

- **What are two ways to praise God in church?** Prayer and music.
- **Exactly how do we give praise to God through our prayers?** By thanking Him and telling Him that we love Him.
- **Why is it important to praise God?** Because we have so much to be thankful for! God is our Creator; He made *everything*, including the earth itself; He has given us eternal life through His sacrifice on the cross.

Divide students into groups of three to five and distribute "He Deserves Our Praise!" and pens or pencils. Instruct students to follow the directions on the handout, completing the first part on their own and using the second part for discussion within their small groups. If there is time, have groups share some of their responses with the whole group.

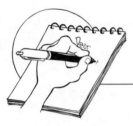

Higher Ground

Worshiping God is an interactive experience.

Lesson from the Grandstands

Materials Needed: Two copies of "Lesson from the Grandstands" (pp. 83-84), a table and two chairs.

Preparation: Set up the table and chairs in restaurant style.

Ask students to think about what it means to praise God. Recruit two volunteers (a boy and a girl) to play the parts of Kathy and Jeff in "Lesson from the Grandstands." Give each volunteer a copy of the skit and let the acting begin!

When the award-winning drama is through and the roaring applause dies down, share the following statement and questions from a real teenager:

> **I'm a Christian. I attend church regularly. I've accepted Jesus as my Savior. I went to the altar during winter retreat and prayed the sinner's prayer. It was a great experience, but I've never really recaptured that feeling since then.**
>
> **Honestly, after that night I didn't know what to do. I pray sometimes, but does God really hear my prayers? How should I pray? And where does the Bible fit in?**

Explain: **Many who become Christians have the same problems. After committing their lives to Jesus Christ, they just don't know what to do. How would you respond if this person asked for your advice?**

Allow time for discussion, making sure to encourage students' responses.

Revolution Time

God wants us to treat worship as a priority in our lives.

High Voltage Worship

Materials Needed: Copies of "How to Be a High-Voltage Christian" (p. 85) and "Worship, Not Work/Praise God!" (p. 86).

Explain: **Worshiping and praising God is an interactive experience. James 4:8 says "Come near to God and he will come near to you." Worship is both public and private, involving our heads and our hearts. Worship builds us into stronger Christians; as we linger in God's presence, praising Him, it's like getting a high-voltage spiritual** *zap*!

Continue: **Each one of us is an awesome creation of God—and He wants our praise and worship. It pleases Him when we plug our lives into the ultimate Power Source—and when we stay plugged in, those high-voltage spiritual** *zaps* **will gradually transform us into high-voltage Christians! Making worship a priority is a choice we have to make; if we choose not to give worship the place it demands in our lives, our Christian walk will be ineffective and shallow—and definitely not the walk with God that He wants to take with us.**

Distribute "Worship, Not Work/Praise God!" Discuss the section of the handout titled "Worship, Not Work" and then direct students' attention to the section titled "Praise God!" and end the meeting using the outline as a group prayer. If you have time, consider singing a worship song or two! Before students leave, give "How to Be a High-Voltage Christian" to each one. Challenge them to take the handout home and *do it*.

Let's Talk

He Deserves Our Praise!

Rate Your Worship

Individual Activity

Write T (True) or F (False) to rate your worship.

_____ My interest in faith is equal to other interests in my life, such as relationships with the opposite sex, sports, music, etc.

_____ The services at my church bore me to death.

_____ Sometimes I go weeks without praying.

_____ God often seems distant to me.

If you answered true to *any* of these questions, take a few moments to consider whether or not God really is the most important person in your life. Ask yourself:

- Am I allowing other pursuits to push God out of my life?
- Is church really boring or am I just too tired to participate?
- Do I expect God to communicate with me without any effort on my part?
- Am I just going through the motions when I pray?

Powerful and Effective Communication

Group Discussion

1. What kind of worshiper does God seek? (See John 4:19-26.)
2. How can friends make or break you?
3. What are some of the qualities that make Jesus the ultimate best friend? (See John 15:9-17.)

Is any one of you in trouble? He should pray. Is anyone happy? Let him sing songs of praise. Is any one of you sick? He should call the elders of the church to pray over him and anoint him with oil in the name of the Lord. And the prayer offered in faith will make the sick person well; the Lord will raise him up. If he has sinned, he will be forgiven. Therefore confess your sins to each other and pray for each other so that you may be healed. The prayer of a righteous man is powerful and effective. James 5:13-16

Lesson from the Grandstands

The scene opens as two teenagers are sitting in a fast-food restaurant enjoying their French fries and sodas.

Kathy: What do you mean you don't want to come to youth group tonight?! You promised you would this time.

Jeff takes a sip of soda, eats some French fries and then looks across the table at Kathy.

Jeff: I just don't get into all that singing and clapping and lifting up your hands—you know, *all* of that stuff your youth pastor tells everybody to do.

Kathy: (*Looking irritated.*) It's called "worship," Jeff.

Jeff: Yeah, well, whatever . . . it's not my style. Why can't you accept me the way I am? I'll follow God my way; you do it your way. (*Leans forward.*) Look, I went to that winter retreat just because you asked me to. I even accepted Jesus in my life and prayed with you! And that was great. Then you and I started dating—and that was even better. I just don't need to go to a church, OK? (*Reaches for Kathy's hand.*) But I do need you.

Kathy: (*Yanks her hand away.*) Don't you see how twisted that is, Jeff? You don't just say a few magic words to God and then go off and do what you want. Your commitment to Jesus has to be real. You have to mean it—and live it. And live it His way—not yours.

Jeff: (*Rolls his eyes.*) Oh, great. Here comes your youth pastor's favorite guilt-filled sermon. (*Flops back in his chair.*) I've heard it before, you know. Read my lips: I just don't fit your neat, little mold of how a Christian is supposed to act. (*Pauses and fidgets with his soda.*) I'm not a phony, Kathy. My faith *is* as real as yours.

Kathy: Fine, Jeff—then grow it! I'm not forcing you to fit a mold. How about the soccer games you watch?

Jeff: Soccer?! What?

Kathy: Soccer, basketball, hockey—whatever. The point is that you never miss a game on TV. And when you watch a game, you raise your arms and scream for your favorite team, right?

Jeff: (*Shrugs.*) Yeah, I guess so.

Kathy: You also get excited when you go to concerts. You yell and sing and dance around, right?

Jeff: (*Sheepishly.*) Yeah.

Kathy: You even flatter me with kind words and tell me how much you love me.

Jeff: (*Grins.*) And I mean it! But what does this have to do with faith?

Kathy: (*Smiles.*) Glad you asked! You do all of this for everything important in your life—except God. If you love Jesus as much as you do sports or music—or me—then show it.

Jeff looks shocked and puzzled as he imagines dancing around and yelling during a youth leader's talk.

Kathy: *(Knowing what Jeff is imagining.)* No, silly, you don't have to scream and jump around at church. Do it in your heart when you pray. Tell Jesus how much you love Him. Thank Him for all the stuff He's done in your life. It's not that hard or mysterious. It's really pretty simple. Praying and praising God is as easy as talking to me.

Jeff: *(Relaxes and smiles).* Good sermon, Kath! No guilt. I'll start praying more. I'll go to youth group with you tonight. I guess I'll give this God thing a chance.

How to Be a High-Voltage Christian

Get Wired

Commit to spending some time alone with God this week. Carve out a block of quiet time every day for prayer. Exactly what time you do this and for how long is up to you.

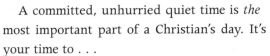

Find a private place—your bedroom, sitting at the kitchen table after everyone else is asleep, an undisturbed corner of your school's library—*anywhere*! The key is to give God your undivided attention.

A committed, unhurried quiet time is *the* most important part of a Christian's day. It's your time to . . .

- Let go of your fears and worries.
- Listen to God's instruction.
- Praise your awesome creator.
- Pray for friends and family.
- Power up with the Holy Spirit.

Stay Plugged In

Commit to attending church services. True, not every church service will be filled with fireworks—not even in *your church*—but you can make worship more meaningful by doing two simple things.

- Ask God to prepare your heart *before* you step through the church doors. Tell Him that you really want to focus on Him and deepen your faith.
- Ask God to help you make knowing Him *the* priority in your life. This means spending time reading the Bible and praying and worshiping Him daily.

Worship, Not Work

As you worship God, you *should* **. . .**
- Give Him your praise and glory.
- Give Him your thanks.
- Give Him your whole heart.

As you worship God, you should *not* **. . .**
- Go through the motions of a ritual without thinking about what it means.
- Approach Him with wrong motives, using your praise as a means of getting something.
- Treat this special time as if it's an *option*!

Praise God!

Follow the leader and glory be to the Lord!

Leader: Lord, we have so much to celebrate! You love us with an undying love.

Group: PRAISE God in His sanctuary!

Leader: Lord, You've forgiven us.

Group: PRAISE Him in His mighty heavens!

Leader: Lord, You won the victory.

Group: PRAISE Him for His acts of power.

Leader: Lord, we have so much to celebrate: Moms and Dads; brothers and sisters; chocolate chip cookies; wildflowers; laughter; pounding waves; bare feet squishing in sand; peace, purpose, life!

All: We PRAISE You, Lord, for Your surpassing greatness.

Repent

The Message

Repentance results in God's forgiveness.

Key Verse

"From that time on Jesus began to preach, 'Repent, for the kingdom of heaven is near.'" Matthew 4:17

Biblical Basis

Psalm 51:1-7; Matthew 4:17; 6:9-13; Mark 1:15; Romans 6:1-14

Power Up

The choices we make—big and small—all matter to God.

Voices and Choices

Materials Needed: Several Bibles and candy for prizes.

Welcome students and explain: **As we face choices in our daily lives, we hear many different voices trying to influence our tough decisions.**

Divide the group in half and designate one group as Temptation and the other as Light. Instruct students to form two walls, standing shoulder-to-shoulder, each wall facing the other with a path through the middle.

Ask for a volunteer to stand at one end of the path between the walls. As he or she walks down the path, students in the Temptation wall will try to entice the walker to their side by promising happiness in sin; students forming the Light wall will quote Scripture to convince the walker to follow God and obey His commands. As he or she proceeds down the path, the walker must continually choose sides.

Allow a few minutes for the walker to follow the path; then explain that in life, every time we choose to sin matters to God. Repentance is what He desires when we choose to follow temptation over His will for us.

Divide students into small groups of four to six and distribute Bibles. Determine a time limit and instruct students to wait for your signal before they race to find Scripture verses dealing with or directly mentioning repentance. (The story of David and Bathsheba is one example of a story that deals with repentance without mentioning it by name.) Give the signal. When the time is up, determine which group found the most references and award candy to the winning group.

Explain: **Repentance is hard work and well worth it. Don't repent just to be on God's good side or to make yourself look holy in front of your friends. Do it because you want your relationship with God to be real. It's also important to recognize the danger of unchecked sin in your life; you can't move forward in your Christian walk if you're covering up sin. It's best to deal with it now, because it will eventually surface. The choice is yours.**

Solid Truth

Repentance is necessary for our walk with Jesus.

The Choice Is Yours

Materials Needed: Several Bibles, copies of "Let's Talk" (p. 92) and pens or pencils.

Distribute Bibles and ask a volunteer to read Matthew 4:17; then discuss:

Why is it important for us to confess our sins to Jesus? So that He can forgive us and help us to grow stronger in our faith.

What does it mean to repent? To stop doing, saying or thinking something that's bad and to begin obeying Jesus.

Ask a volunteer to read Psalm 51:1-7 and another to read Romans 6:1-14. After the verses have been read, share the following confession of an imaginary teen:

> Last year I wrote the answers to a chemistry test on my hand. Since then it's been easy to do again and again. I'm not saying I feel good about cheating, because I feel incredibly guilty all the time. I know what I'm doing is wrong, but I can't seem to stop. What's worse, I'm a Christian and some kids look up to me at church. Can God help me overcome my temptation and turn back to Him? I feel like I can't look at myself in the mirror, much less face God in prayer.

Point out that all of God's children face choices and that the choices we make define who we are. Divide students into groups of four to six; then distribute "Repentance or Repeated Sin?" and pens or pencils. Instruct students to complete the handouts individually; then discuss their answers within their small groups.

Ask students to bow their heads; then lead them through the following prayer:

> Lord, please forgive me for not repenting of sins in my life. I know they are wrong and draw me away from close fellowship with You, but I can't seem to break free. Show me how to live a life of repentance—a life of love toward You. Help me to be aware of things that would rob me of my relationship with You. Amen.

Higher Ground

God forgives our sin and restores our lives.

Moral Dilemma Snapshots

Materials Needed: Copies of "Moral Dilemma Snapshots" (p. 93).

Divide students into three groups. As you distribute "Moral Dilemma Snapshots," explain that the three snapshot scenarios are about real Christian teenagers. Assign each group one of the dilemmas and instruct groups to read their assigned dilemma and discuss: **How did these Christian teens get tangled up in sin?** Then have each group come up with a solution/ending to the problem. If there is time, have each group share its ending.

Explain: **Just as it's impossible to drive a car in two directions at the same time—**

you have to choose a path—so it is in your walk with Christ. You're either moving toward Him or you're not; it's your choice. Only when you choose to follow God can you experience peace in knowing that you're obeying Him.

The dictionary says that to repent is "to turn from sin and dedicate oneself to the amendment of one's life."[1] Once a person is deeply involved in a sin, it can be really difficult to see the way out—and even more difficult to turn back to the way God wants. No matter how hard that critical step might be, though, we *have* to resist giving into the temptation to do what we want and consciously make the choice to follow God's way.

Discuss: So, if we change our ways and turn from sin, what's the point of repentance in prayer—why do we have to go over the whole thing with God?

Explain: The wall of sin that we've built between us and God is broken down when we are specific in confessing our sins. When we confess all ungodly thoughts, words or deeds to God and tell Him that we're truly sorry for the sins we've committed, we experience a change of attitude *and* we can rely on God's strength to turn away from sin.

Revolution Time

We are completely responsible for our own actions—and equally responsible for our repentance.

Search Your Soul

Materials Needed: Copies of "Get Right, Get Going!" (p. 94).

Distribute "Get Right, Get Going!" and invite students to read through the handout, considering how each of the questions might apply to their particular situations. Encourage students to keep the handout and reflect upon the questions frequently as a reminder to keep their lives on track—the *right* track.

Close the meeting in prayer, emphasizing how we all must yield to God. **Suggestion:** Try a responsive prayer. Call out to God with a line of prayer, then have students repeat that line. For example, pray Christ's instruction on prayer from Matthew 6:9-13:

Leader:	**Our Father in heaven, hallowed be your name.**
All:	Our Father in heaven, hallowed be your name.
Leader:	**Your kingdom come, your will be done on earth as it is in heaven.**
All:	Your kingdom come, your will be done on earth as it is in heaven.
Leader:	**Give us today our daily bread.**
All:	Give us today our daily bread.
Leader:	**Forgive us our debts, as we also have forgiven our debtors.**
All:	Forgive us our debts, as we also have forgiven our debtors.

Leader: **And lead us not into temptation, but deliver us from the evil one.**

All: And lead us not into temptation, but deliver us from the evil one.

Leader: **Amen.**

Note
1. *Merriam-Webster's Collegiate Dictionary*, 10th ed., s.v. "repent."

Let's Talk

Repentance or Repeated Sin?

Answer the following questions to discover where you stand:

1. Do you allow any repeated sins in your life? If so, what are they?

2. What is the most important thing in your life right now?

3. Why should you repent if you're already a Christian?

4. Have you isolated yourself from other believers to hide your sin? If so, in what ways?

5. If you're serious about walking with God, what's your next step?

These are pretty tough questions to answer honestly, but each one of them has a purpose: God wants to be first in your life. He thinks sin is serious stuff—so serious that He sent His Son to die on the cross as payment for your sins. He knew you were hopeless and helpless without Him, so He came down to Earth for you.

When you choose to follow Christ, you choose to see things from His perspective. Regarding sin, He wants you to continually repent—to turn away from it; in doing so, you run back into the arms of your loving Savior and your relationship with Him is once again where it needs to be.

Moral Dilemma Snapshots

Scenario One

Josh lands a job at Wal-Mart, helping to keep the stockroom in order. The regular employees seem pretty cool, and he makes friends with a couple of guys his age.

A few weeks into his job, Paul, one of Josh's new coworkers, motions for him to help stack several boxes of electronics. While they're working, Paul asks, "Hey Josh, do you have a CD player?"

"No," Josh answers. "I asked for one for Christmas, but I'm not holding my breath; my parents are broke."

"Well, you don't have to wait for Christmas, Josh, old pal. Here, grab one of these; it'll fit right into your jacket."

Josh is stunned. "Hey, that's stealing. I can't do that."

"Take it," insists Paul. "It's not like it's really stealing. All of this stuff is going back to the Wal-Mart warehouse. Nobody will know. Nobody even cares—in fact, I'm sure they even budget for it!"

Josh reluctantly slips the CD player into his pocket, but deep in the pit of his stomach he knows it is wrong.

Scenario Two

It's staring right at her. It's so easy to see. The answers to the math test are lying right there on the desk belonging to Mr. Math Genius—who after flying right through the test, disappeared to use the restroom.

Tanya is *so* tempted; the teacher is busy grading papers and no one's looking. *I so need to get a good grade on this test. This could solve my problems*, she tells herself, keeping an eye on the teacher. *I know it's cheating, but it's only this once—just to get me back on my feet. Besides, I know this stuff; I'm just having an off day.*

Tanya caves in and begins to frantically jot down the answers. *I know this isn't right, but I didn't have time to study last night because of soccer practice and then I had to go to youth group.*

Scenario Three

It's springtime and love is in the air. Danny is head-over-heels *crazy* about Susan. She's bright, beautiful and loves to cuddle—the perfect girlfriend. As far as sex goes, the two have made a pact for purity: "We're waiting until marriage."

Weeks turn into months and Danny and Susan are spending more and more time alone, and less and less time in God's Word. One evening, while Susan's parents are away, what begins as an innocent kiss leads to a passionate one. That's when it happens— exactly what they vowed not to do.

In the weeks and months that follow, the once-happy couple finds their relationship shifting from a foundation of faith to one preoccupied with sex. The time they enjoyed before seems like an eternity away, and it's not long before the fun fades and the reality of their new relationship sets in. The lack of the quality time they used to spend together—talking, laughing, studying God's Word—pushes Danny and Susan further apart and they grow bitter toward each other. Eventually, their relationship ends in a painful breakup; and even worse, their faith is damaged in the process.

Get Right, Get Going!

The kingdom of God is near. Repent and believe the good news.
Mark 1:15

Is there anything in your life that does *not* bring glory to God? If so, what are you going to do about it? Write some ideas below.

Think back to the story about Danny and Susan from "Moral Dilemma Snapshots." Instead of giving in to the temptation to become physically intimate, what if they had listened to God's calling and recognized that the urge was too overwhelming to stay together? Their broken relationship would have hurt both of them, but their bond with Christ would have remained strong and they wouldn't have lost their sexual purity.

Making a decision that honors God—even when it sacrifices what you want—is repentance *in action*.

You are responsible for your actions—no one else. If you're involved in something you know you shouldn't be, confess it to God. Next, tell a parent or youth pastor and take steps to stop your involvement.

What if Christ were to return for His Church tonight? Would you be ashamed of what He caught you doing? If so, *change* your behavior and *obey* Him. It's the best decision you'll ever make.

Ask

The Message

God wants to hear our hearts' desires.

Key Verses

"Ask and it will be given to you; seek and you will find; knock and the door will be opened to you. For everyone who asks receives; he who seeks finds; and to him who knocks, the door will be opened." Matthew 7:7,8

Biblical Basis

Psalm 46:10; Proverbs 14:12; Matthew 7:7,8; 11:29,30; John 14:18; 15:7,9; Romans 8:26,27; Ephesians 6:18; Philippians 4:4-7; Revelation 2:7,11,17,26; 3:5,12,20,21

Power Up

God knows what's best for us.

Eternal Perspective

Materials Needed: A *long* piece of rope (at least 28 feet!), room to stretch out the rope, a measuring tape and three permanent felt-tip pens: one green, one red and one black.

Preparation: Use the markers and measuring tape to mark the rope as follows: Place a large *green dot* directly in the middle; a *red dot* exactly 10 inches to the right of the green one; and place two *black lines*—one inch apart—exactly 10 inches to the right of the red dot (20 inches to the right of the green one).

Welcome students and ask for two volunteers to hold the rope at each end (you'll need to hold up the middle). Explain that the rope represents eternity, the green dot symbolizes creation, and the red dot stands for Christ's sacrifice on the cross. Ask students to guess what the black lines indicate. Allow for some guessing; then explain: **These lines symbolize your life—your *entire* life here on Earth. From an eternal perspective, it seems pretty short, doesn't it? Although we live in this world and are subject to the laws of time and space, God lives totally outside of these laws. To Him, a thousand years could be like an instant.**

Sometimes when we take our requests to God in prayer, it may seem as if it takes forever for Him to answer—and even when we finally *get* our answer, it's not what we had hoped it would be. It's important to keep in mind that God knows what's best for us from an *eternal* perspective. We base our decisions on our extremely limited time on Earth; God bases His on eternity.

Open in prayer, focusing on trusting God and His eternal perspective.

Solid Truth

God listens to and answers all of our prayers.

Materials Needed: Several Bibles, copies of "Let's Talk" (p. 99) and pens or pencils.

Distribute Bibles and ask a volunteer to read Matthew 7:7,8; then briefly discuss:

What kinds of things will God give us when we pray—will he give Ryan the new roller blades he wants so badly? God isn't in the Santa business. What He *will* give us is everything that's best for us.

What does knocking on a door have to do with prayer? Knocking on a door means to go to God and to ask Him about everything that's on our minds.

What should we do when we pray over and over again for something and it seems as if God's not answering? Continue to pray and to trust, ask God if there's something else that you should pray for, talk to a trusted adult about your prayer request.

Divide students into small groups of four to six and distribute "Let's Talk" and pens or pencils. Instruct students to complete handouts and then discuss their answers within their small groups.

Allow several minutes for small-group discussion; then lead students through the following prayer:

> Lord, help me to trust that You will meet my needs. Teach me how to pray—how to take every need to You. Lord, teach me how to ask in prayer. Give me an extra measure of peace that You're protecting me—and that You'll do the right thing in every situation. I'm taking Your hand right now—and I'm trusting You. Amen.

Higher Ground

God helps us in times of need.

Where Are You, God?

Materials Needed: Copies of "Where Are You, God?" (p. 100).

Preparation: Arrange for a student to play the part of the teen in the skit and give him or her a copy of "Where Are You, God?" to study. (*You* will play the part of Jesus, so prepare and memorize your lines to use the skit to bring home your message in a powerful way.)

Explain: Did you ever think that God might be upset if you told Him how you really feel? Guess what? God already knows *everything* **about you—even your sinful nature. Yet He still loves you and wants you to experience His love, forgiveness and power in** *all* **areas of your life.**

Introduce the skit, briefly highlighting that it's about a totally stressed-out teenager. Perform the skit; then discuss:

At the beginning of the skit, what did this person think about his or her time to pray?

How did his or her thoughts change?

Can you relate to this experience? How have your experiences in prayer been similar or different?

Revolution Time

We should never be afraid to talk to God about anything!

Materials Needed: Copies of "Ask Away" (p. 101) and pens or pencils.

Explain: **We can freely call upon God for absolutely anything! Got a secret? Feeling depressed? Need some answers? You can share** *anything* **with God and ask for His help. His Word promises He will listen—and answer!**

If you ask for something, you may be told no. There is always that chance. But if you *don't* **ask, you will definitely** *never* **hear yes! This is true in life—and in prayer. Jesus wants us to approach Him with boldness. He wants us take every request to Him—to pour out our hearts to Him. Are you afraid to approach Jesus with your needs? Are you afraid to ask? Why?**

Distribute "Ask Away" and pens or pencils; then instruct students to take a few minutes to seriously consider the handout questions.

Allow enough time for students to complete their handouts; then close the session in prayer, thanking Jesus for always listening and for always knowing what is best for us.
Optional: Invite students to call out to God in prayer; praying aloud for one another, their friends and families, schools, etc.

Let's Talk

Approaching Jesus Through Prayer

1. Who is your closest friend and what helped you develop the close relationship you have with him or her?

2. Developing a close relationship with God involves . . .

3. Read Revelation 2:7,11,17,26; 3:5,12,21. What do these verses tell you about the kind of character God wants to develop in us?

4. What is prayer and why is it important to pray? (Stumped? Check out Romans 8:26,27; Ephesians 6:18; Philippians 4:4-7 and Revelation 3:20.)

5. What makes the Bible different from other collections of books?

6. Why do you think the Bible and prayer go hand in hand?

7. Does Jesus hear every single one of our prayers? How do you know?

8. Will Jesus always answer our prayers by giving us what we want? Why or why not?

Where Are You, God?

Teen: (*Slams his Bible shut and lowers his head.*) Lord, I don't have time to pray. I've got too much to do: a huge math test to study for, a history report that's due in two days, band practice after school, chores my mom keeps hounding me about. I can't take it, Lord. There's too much pressure. When am I supposed to have time to pray?

Jesus: (*Peacefully and serenely standing just behind Teen's shoulder.*) "Be still and know that I am God."[1]

Teen: I know I have a bunch of stuff to confess. I feel so guilty about yelling at my mom yesterday and then I took out my anger on my little brother. Lord, I just can't take it anymore. There's just too much pressure. I don't have time to do this. (*Looks up toward ceiling.*) H-e-l-l-o up there!? Are You really listening?

Jesus: "Take my yoke upon you and learn from me, for I am gentle and humble in heart, and you will find rest for your souls. For my yoke is easy and my burden is light."[2]

Teen: And another thing. (*Talking to ceiling.*) Where are You, God? Do You really care about me?

Jesus: "I will not leave you as orphans; I will come to you."[3]

Teen: Lord, being a Christian isn't easy—especially when I see how my non-Christian friends' lives are going great! Their lives seem so simple.

Jesus: "There is a way that seems right to a man, but in the end it leads to death."[4]

Teen: Oh, Lord. Who am I trying to kid? Even though all this faith stuff gets hard and confusing, I know I need You. I know I need to follow You. (*Bows head.*) Will You help me? Will You clear away some of the confusion and help me to grow closer to You?

Jesus: "If you remain in me and my words remain in you, ask whatever you wish, and it will be given you. . . . As the Father has loved me, so have I loved you."[5]

Teen: (*Stands and smiles.*) It's kinda weird. I'm so stressed out, and I don't have time for anything—but I'm glad I prayed. (*Looks at Bible.*) Somehow, I think I just encountered Jesus. It's amazing: this faith thing really works. (*Looks up again.*) OK, God. Tomorrow—same place, same time. (*Teen exits and Jesus follows.*)

Notes
1. Psalm 46:10
2. Matthew 11:29,30
3. John 14:18
4. Proverbs 14:12
5. John 15:7,9

Ask Away

Ask

Are you still crawling and clawing and inching your way through life? Do you feel like a shell of someone who's just wasting away? Are you facing major rejection everywhere you turn? Don't let that stop you. Jesus is right here, right now—stretching out His hand to you. Take it! He's offering you freedom and forgiveness and a whole new life with Him.

Understand

There are four absolute, undeniable truths:

1. You can't swim against the tide of God and survive. But you can come to the surface and cry out "Abba, Father," and He'll set you on the right course.
2. Not one person on this planet is outside the reach of God's love.
3. Even if you can't begin to fathom the depth of your sin, Jesus understands—and He forgives you.
4. God answers every single one of our prayers.

Trust

Take Jesus at His word; when He says something, it happens! Maybe not right away or exactly when we want it to, but in God's time, it will happen. When God says that you're forgiven, unload the guilt. When He says you're valuable, believe Him! When He says you're provided for, lay aside the worry. And when He says to come to Him in prayer about all things—big or small—DO IT!

Yield

The Message

To yield means to obey God.

Key Verse

"Submit yourselves, then, to God. Resist the devil, and he will flee from you." James 4:7

Biblical Basis

Genesis 22:2,9-12,17,18; John 10:10,17,18; 15:4,5; James 1:22-25; 4:7

Power Up

God wants to guide our steps and bless our lives.

The Voice That Guides

Materials Needed: Two blindfolds, a large roll of masking tape, candy for prizes, two referees (adult volunteers).

Preparation: Use the tape to create two curvy, wacky paths (with lots of sharp turns) and a finish line at the end.

Welcome students and divide them into two teams. Ask for three volunteers from each team and assign them the following roles: One from each team will be the Voice That Guides; one from each team will be the Voice That Destroys; and one from each team will be Humanity.

Here are the rules for the game: The two students representing Humanity are going to race through the course. The first one who makes it to the finish line *without touching or crossing over the lines* wins candy for his or her team. If Humanity steps on or over the line, he or she must start over. Simple, right? *Wrong!* (There's always a catch for youth games!) Humanity will be blindfolded and will be directed by the Voice That Guides from his or her *own team*—the guide will walk alongside and give directions for maneuvering the course and steering clear of the masking-tape lines. The Voice That Destroys from the *opposing team* will also walk alongside, attempting to direct Humanity the wrong way.

Blindfold the two students representing Humanity; then give the signal to begin the race. Encourage each team to cheer for its representative. Reward candy to the team that completes the course in the least time. Discuss:

How is this path like the one we face in life? We often have to steer clear of things that can hurt us: the temptation to lie or steal, other people who can talk us into doing bad things.

What happens when we listen to the Voice That Destroys? We have problems and sometimes even get hurt.

Jesus Christ is our Voice That Guides. How do we tune in His voice? Through prayer, by attending church, Bible study.

Solid Truth

It's not enough to believe in God; we must submit our lives to Him.

Submit Yourself

Materials Needed: Several Bibles, copies of "Let's Talk" (p. 107) and pens or pencils.

Distribute Bibles and ask a volunteer to read James 4:7; then explain: **The Bible is clear about what yielding to God is all about.** Ask another volunteer to read John 15:4,5, and another to read James 1:22-25.

Explain: **Some Christians commit their lives to Christ and then live however they please. Consider what Christ went through to purchase your life for eternity. He** *chose* **to yield to the Father's plan for the redemption of humanity. He made a way for you and me to get to heaven.** Read John 10:17,18; then continue: **We can't begin to understand what it must have been like to be betrayed, beaten, ridiculed and crucified—not because Jesus did anything wrong, but for the sins of others. Christ endured all that and more to give you the chance to know** *and obey* **Him, as He obeyed His Father.**

Divide students into small groups of four to six and distribute "Let's Talk" and pens or pencils. Instruct groups to discuss the questions and encourage students to take notes in the spaces provided. Allow several minutes for the discussion; then lead students through the following prayer:

> **Lord, help us yield to You in every area of our lives. Help us see that You desire to guide us by Your Word. You truly care about us and want only the best for us. Thank You for Your love for us. Amen.**

Higher Ground

We must pay attention to the alarms God sets off in our lives.

Running on Empty

Materials Needed: Copies of "Unheeded Warnings" (p. 108).

Explain: **God sets off all kinds of alarms and warning signs in our lives; it's up to us to tune in and take action. If we don't, we run the risk of a serious attack from Satan. Let's take a look at someone who didn't pay attention to the warning signs.**

Distribute "Unheeded Warnings" and ask several volunteers to take turns reading the story (have them switch after each paragraph). After the story has been read, discuss:

What did Jordan learn through this? To be aware of the warning signs—heard, seen and felt!

What are some warning lights that God gives us to watch for? Neglecting prayer, situations that put us in positions of being tempted to sin, etc.

Was there ever a time when you ignored God's instructions and ended up regretting it? (Allow volunteers to share, but don't put anyone on the spot.)

Explain: **There are yield signs everywhere we drive, telling us to watch for and yield to oncoming traffic. Many accidents happen simply because someone failed to obey the yield sign—not because they didn't see it or read it, but because they didn't *obey* it. The same principle applies to life; when you're racing down the road of life and you see a sign telling you what to do, you have a choice. For a Christian, that sign represents Scripture. You can either heed the sign's instruction or ignore it and risk your spiritual safety.**

The next time you see a yield sign next to the road, remember that God has given you His Word to guide you. Traffic laws don't enforce themselves and neither do spiritual warning signs. It's our choice to read and heed!

Revolution Time

God forgives as when we fail and sin.

Cross It Out

Materials Needed: Copies of "Remain in Him" (p. 109), pens or pencils, 3x5-inch index cards, thumbtacks, a hammer, nails and two two-by-fours (one slightly shorter than the other). **Low-tech option:** Substitute paper for the wood, and tape for the nails and thumbtacks.

 Preparation: Build a cross with the two-by-fours (or draw one on paper); then place the cross at the front of the meeting room.

Distribute an index card, a thumbtack (or a piece of tape) and a pen or pencil to each student. Instruct them to write down one thing they are currently struggling with (let them know that they don't have to put their names on the cards). Areas of struggle could include failing to honor God, not trusting Him to take over a certain area of their lives, etc.

Allow time for students to write; then lead them in the following prayer:

> **Lord, I need Your help to overcome and give to You this thing I've written down. Help me to see You as my Redeemer and Helper. Give me the strength to submit to You. Amen.**

Explain: **When Jesus died on the cross, He took on all of our sins. He forgave us and wiped our slates clean. He wants us to bring everything in our lives to Him at the cross. He desires to take on our burdens and guide us on our paths.**

Invite students to come forward and secure their cards to the cross with the thumbtacks.

Distribute "Remain in Him" and encourage students to read it often during the upcoming week to remind them to give their lives to God and yield to His will.

Dim the lights in the room (you'll want enough light to keep an eye on everyone; after all, they *are* teens and prone to pranks!) and have everyone kneel. Spend a few moments in silent prayer to close the session.

Let's Talk

Who's in Control?

Read the following account of Moses' complete obedience to God from Genesis 22:2,9-12,17,18:

> *"Take your son, your only son, Isaac, whom you love, and go to the region of Moriah. Sacrifice him there as a burnt offering on one of the mountains I will tell you about."*
>
> *When they reached the place God had told him about, Abraham built an altar there and arranged the wood on it. He bound his son Isaac and laid him on the altar, on top of the wood. Then he reached out his hand and took the knife to slay his son. But the angel of the LORD called out to him from heaven, "Abraham! Abraham!"*
>
> *"Here I am," he replied.*
>
> *"Do not lay a hand on the boy," he said. "Do not do anything to him. Now I know that you fear God, because you have not withheld from me your son, your only son.*
>
> *"I will surely bless you and make your descendants as numerous as the stars in the sky and as the sand on the seashore. Your descendants will take possession of the cities of their enemies, and through your offspring all nations on earth will be blessed, because you have obeyed me."*

Discuss in your small group:

1. God asked Abraham to commit an unthinkable act. How would you feel if you were in Abraham's place?

2. What gave Abraham the strength to obey God?

3. What should you do the next time you're faced with the dilemma to obey or not to obey?

Unheeded Warnings

Running late for school—again—16-year-old Jordan hopped into his Toyota pickup and slammed the door. Jamming the key into the ignition, he twisted it abruptly, anxious to be on his way. The engine grumbled a few times, coughed and sputtered and finally roared to life. *I wonder what that rattle is,* he thought. *Oh, forget it. It's just the cold weather. Besides, it's an old truck; it's always making some weird noise.*

Jordan yanked the gearshift into reverse and screeched out of the driveway, missing the mailbox by an inch. Throwing the gear into drive, he stomped on the pedal and thundered down the street. As he glanced in the rearview mirror, he saw white smoke begin to pour out of the tailpipe. *Must be colder out than I thought.*

He checked the speedometer to make sure he wasn't going too fast. *Forty-five. Not bad,* he thought, *but I should probably slow down. Dad will kill me if I get another ticket.*

Suddenly, a warning light next to the speedometer began to blink. A red light—the one with the picture of a tiny oil can. It had first winked at him a week ago, but he kept forgetting to add oil. Last night his dad had insisted that he take care of it. "You'll be sorry if you don't" echoed in Jordan's ears; and he promised himself to get right on it after school, reasoning, *I can't afford to stop now. I'm too late as it is.*

Jordan turned on his new stereo. It took several seconds for the amplifiers to warm up, but when they did, the entire pickup vibrated to the music and he happily drummed on the steering wheel and sang along.

While he was enjoying his music, Jordan noticed that the smoke coming from the truck was getting worse. He checked the temperature gauge—the truck was *hot*. Although he was hitting the gas, the truck was slowing down. Frantically, he switched off the radio—no engine noise. He guided the truck off to the side of the street, shifted into park and turned off the ignition. Closing his eyes, Jordan reached for his keys and twisted the ignition. *Please, oh please, start. C'mon. C'mon.* It was no use; his metallic-blue pride and joy just wouldn't turn over.

A wave of nausea swept through Jordan's stomach as he realized what had happened; the lack of oil seized the engine. He put his head on the steering wheel, thinking *Dad's never gonna let me drive again. How am I going to tell him about this?*

Remain in Him

Yield your time to God every day.

Before you can expect to have knowledge and strength to submit to God, you have to know Him. Submitting the first part of your day is a great way to show Him your love and devotion. Start with just five minutes every morning before school. Read the Scriptures, pray, listen and thank Him for His many blessings. Once you make this a habit, obeying God will become second nature. If you miss a day, then start over and keep going.

Examine your life.

It's easy to keep secret sins in the closet of your heart. It's easy to pretend that no one knows about them. But God not only knows, He also wants to clean up those dark places and bring them into the light of His Word. You can't be a part-time Christian and expect to be productive. It's an all-or-nothing deal to be a servant of Christ.

Talk to God about any areas of your life you're not proud of. He already knows all your hurts. He's waiting for you to bring them to Him.

Read 1 John 1:9 and see what God does with the ugly things in your life when you confess and repent. Yield to Him, and He will set you free.

I have come that they may have life, and
have it to the full. John 10:10

Putting Prayer into Practice

The Message

God wants us to make prayer a priority—especially when it comes to sharing the gospel with non-Christians.

Key Verse

"And call upon me in the day of trouble; I will deliver you, and you will honor me." Psalm 50:15

Biblical Basis

Psalm 50:15; Jeremiah 1:4-9; John 1:12; Romans 3:23; Ephesians 4:2; 1 Peter 3:18; 2 Peter 3:18; 1 John 5:13

For this session, you will need a P.R.A.Y. bracelet for each student. You may order these from the National Day of Prayer Task Force at 800-444-8828.

NOTE

IMPORTANT!

This last session focuses on salvation. Use the following tips to create a long-lasting impression:

- **Allocate extra time for the session.** Allow students plenty of time for searching their hearts, sharing and praying for one another's needs.
- **Invite a strong prayer leader to attend the session.** Ask a well-known pastor or church leader to attend the session and pray with students who want to accept Christ.

MOST IMPORTANTLY!

Invite the Holy Spirit! His work in the lives of those present is what will ultimately effect permanent change. Spend much of your preparation time in prayer. Ask God to draw each student closer to Him. Also, write out a prayer, expressing what you'd like to see accomplished during the session, asking God to do specific things in the life of each student.

Power Up

Faith in God brings hope to the world.

The Light Force

Materials Needed: A flashlight for each student, a big room that can get very dark, candy and lunch bags.

Preparation: Hide the candy in a nearby room that's very dark.

Welcome students to the last session and congratulate them for their perseverance in learning how to P.R.A.Y.! Distribute flashlights and paper bags and inform students that they're going to go on a treasure hunt for some tasty treats. Explain that the flashlights are to stay in the off position until you give the signal and that students will have three minutes once you give the signal to find as much candy as they can. Lead students to the room where you've hidden the candy and let 'em have at it!

After three minutes, signal that it's time for them to stop searching and to return to the meeting room. As students are enjoying their candy (and hopefully sharing), discuss:

How is the dark room similar to the world and the flashlight similar to Jesus? The world is dark with sin. Jesus brings light and hope into the world.

How hard would it have been to find the candy without the flashlight? Very hard—we probably would not have found much at all.

Why do we need Jesus' light in the world? Because He lights the way so that we don't have to stumble around in the darkness, not knowing what path we're on. He guides our steps and blesses our lives.

How do Christians help carry the light of Jesus? Christians lead by example—by Christ's example. His light shines through us when we live as He would have us live.

Solid Truth

We can feel free to ask God for anything according to His will for our lives.

Bear with One Another in Love

Materials Needed: Paper and pens or pencils.

Ask for a show of hands of students who'd like to share something that they need help in taking to God in prayer (again, don't push anyone who isn't comfortable sharing). Allow time for everyone who'd like to share to do so; then ask for two or three volunteers to pray for the needs mentioned, explaining: **Ephesians 4:2 tells us that we are to "be completely humble and gentle; be patient, bearing with one another in love."**

Distribute paper and pens or pencils and invite students to list five ways that they need God's help. Assure them that no one will be asked to share his or her list with you or the rest of the group. Emphasize that a need could be anything from some extra confidence to reconciling with an estranged friend or family member to better communication with parents or teachers. Point out that there is nothing too big or too small to bring before God in prayer.

Higher Ground

God will give us the courage to share our faith.

Scared but Willing

Materials Needed: Several Bibles (one to use in the skit), two copies of "Scared but Willing" (pp. 116-117) and two skateboards.

    Optional Preparation: Recruit two students to play the parts of Josh and Ben and give them copies of the skit, so they have time to practice.

Distribute Bibles and ask a volunteer to read Jeremiah 1:4-9; then introduce the skit by explaining: **Witnessing can be scary, but God promises that he will help us. Let's watch a skit about someone who was scared but willing to be a witness for Jesus.**

    After the skit, award the student actors with plenty of applause; then discuss:

    What holds people back from sharing their faith? Not knowing what to say; fear of rejection, etc.

    How is becoming friends with someone an important step in sharing your faith? Because faith is personal and so is a friendship.

What are some hobbies or interests that can be used to share your faith? (Allow time for students to share their hobbies and interests. This is a great way to get to know more about students for your next group Bible study!)

Revolution Time

Through prayer, we can till the soil and prepare to plant the seeds of salvation in the hearts of others.

Faith Is Serious Business

Materials Needed: Several gift Bibles, copies of "P.R.A.Y." (p. 118), "A Colorful Reminder" (p. 119), P.R.A.Y. bracelets, a white board and a dry-erase marker.

Ask students to share what each letter in P.R.A.Y. stands for. Distribute "P.R.A.Y." and read as a responsive reading.

- **Praise—Celebrate your relationship with Christ.**
  Thank You, Jesus for being my Lord and Savior.
- **Repent—Think about where you have fallen short in thought, word and deed. Then, with a genuine heart, ask for and accept His forgiveness and cleansing.**
  Thank you, Lord, for Your forgiveness. Cleanse my heart, and make me the kind of person You want me to be.
- **Ask—Go to the Savior for help. He is eager to meet your needs!**
  Lord, help me with my problems. Give me the strength, wisdom and courage to face them.
- **Yield—Submit to Christ, understanding that He knows what is best for you.**
  Lord God, I submit my life to You. Call the shots and lead me.

There may still be students in the group who are not yet committed to Christ. Keep this in mind as you are sharing the points on the handout—you may just reach them through this exercise!

NOTE

Explain that the remainder of this session is going to be spent asking God to do some serious work in their lives, focusing on their needs and God's amazing, incredible plan for their salvation.

Ask students to refer to the list they created earlier and to quietly pray for those five areas of their lives using the P.R.A.Y. acronym.

Distribute the P.R.A.Y. bracelets and "A Colorful Reminder" and explain: **Prayer is a critical element to help spread the message of the gospel. Just as a gardener tills the soil before planting the seeds, prayer tills the soil of our hearts to prepare us** for God's message of salvation. When you wear this bracelet, it will serve as a reminder to pray for others and share your faith with them.

NOTE | Use the following information to guide students step-by-step through the colors of the bracelet as outlined on the handout. Where a question is asked, allow for responses before continuing through the directions.

Briefly discuss: **What is sin?** After a few responses, ask a volunteer to identify the first color (black) and read the explanation of how it represents sin; then explain: **When God created Adam and Eve, they enjoyed a personal relationship with Him. Their sin cut them off from His presence and created a huge gulf between all of humanity and God.**

Briefly discuss: **How can we get right with God?** Read the explanation for the color red; then explain: **We** *can't* **get right with God—not without Jesus Christ. He paid the price for our sins by shedding His own blood to atone for them—forgiveness for our sins came through Christ's personal sacrifice.**

Briefly discuss: **What does it mean to be forgiven?** Ask a volunteer to read the explanation for the color white; then explain: **When we accept Jesus Christ into our hearts and turn our lives—sin and all—over to Him, we are washed clean.**

Briefly discuss: **What's eternal life?** Read the explanation for the color gold; then explain: **When we accept Jesus as our Savior, we become brand-new creatures and citizens of heaven.** Explain that, as a citizen of heaven, we still live on Earth, but the earth is no longer our home. We have reserved our place in heaven with God and are assured eternal life with Him.

Briefly discuss: **What does a new life in Christ mean to us right now?** Ask a volunteer to read the explanation for the color green; then explain: **Jesus promises to give us His strength and His love** *right now*. Use the following illustration to drive home the message:

Going through life is like going to the top of a great building. If we choose to live a sinful life and never accept Jesus as our Savior, the sin becomes a dark, rickety, old stairwell that we must climb. We can't ever see the beauty of our lives because we're caught on the stairwell in the dark. Jesus, on the other hand, is like a hand-crafted, beautiful glass elevator, designed to lift us up through our lives. We see the majesty of all of God's creation through the glass, and although life itself may not be perfect, the view and the wonder of it is no longer hidden. The most wonderful thing is that no matter where you are on the stairwell, there's always a door to the elevator. You just have to open it and walk through!

Ask students to bow their heads in prayer and extend an invitation to students who would like to take the opportunity to invite Jesus into their lives to come forward. Lead them in a prayer asking Jesus to be their Lord and Savior and to forgive them and wash them clean from their sins.

After praying with those who come forward, welcome each one by name into God's family and give them the gift Bibles. Encourage the new believers to wear their P.R.A.Y.

bracelets to share the good news with others. (It's also a great idea to write down names and phone numbers for follow-up calls in the next week to encourage new believers to pray regularly, seek God's voice and read His Word as they continue their new journey to spiritual maturity.)

Close in prayer, thanking God for sending His only Son, Jesus Christ, to bridge the gap that sin created. Ask Him to give students courage to share the gospel with their friends and family—even strangers!

Scared but Willing

Characters

Josh, a clean cut, Christian, wearing a P.R.A.Y. bracelet and carrying his skateboard and Bible

Ben, definitely a skater, but not rough looking, carrying his skateboard

Josh standing stage right, Ben stage left, both holding a skateboard. Holding his Bible, Josh approaches the middle of the stage and begins speaking to the audience.

Josh: What?! Me?! Oh sure, I'm just gonna walk right up to some guy—a total skate-boarder—and tell him about Jesus Christ! No way. Anyway, that's what I was think-ing when I first got here. Then I started thinking about some Scripture I heard on Sunday and I knew I *had* to do it. *(Glances at his Bible and then looks up again.)* Maybe you've read it; Jeremiah 1:4-9? The Lord tells us not to use the excuse that we're "just kids." He even promises that He'll be with us and put the words in our mouths. *(Looks over at the skater and then back at the audience.)*

Josh: So there I was. Standing in the middle of a skate park, thinking about sharing my faith with someone else. Believe me, I was scared—but willing. And that's what counts, right? Let me tell you how it happened— *(Returns to stage right as if going back in time.)*

Josh: *(Nervously approaches skater and smiles.)* Hi, I'm Josh. *(Fumbles with his skateboard but manages to stick out his hand.)*

Ben: *(Gives Josh a blank stare; then glances at Bible.)* Ben . . . I'm Ben.

Josh: What I wanted to tell you about is . . . I mean, I was wondering.

Ben stands there—silent, expressionless. He doesn't even seem to blink.

Josh: I was wondering if you knew . . . J-J-Jesus. I mean, do you know Jesus Christ?

Ben looks down, spins a wheel and then shakes his head no.

Josh: No? Well, I just want to say that I'm 15, and I'm a Christian. And it's really cool to follow Jesus. *(Puts down his skateboard, takes a deep breath and holds out his wrist, pointing to his P.R.A.Y. bracelet.)*

Josh: This bracelet represents what I believe. Black stands for sin—your sin keeps you from knowing God. Red represents Christ's blood—Jesus Christ died and rose again so that your sins could be forgiven. White represents how our lives are cleansed from sin—you must also trust Jesus to be your Savior and to forgive you of your sins. Gold stands for eternal life—you have the promise of eternal life with Jesus if you ask Him to be your Lord and Savior.

Ben stops spinning the wheel on his skateboard and even looks half-interested.

Josh: Hey, look, do you want to grab a Coke and talk some more about this?
Ben: *(Smiling.)* OK.

Ben freezes. Josh turns to crowd.

Josh: So that's how it happened. We grabbed a Coke and I became friends with this guy. He asked lots of questions about being a Christian. Unfortunately, he didn't pray to accept Jesus into his heart . . . but I'm praying for him. Well, I'd better go now. Ben and I are gonna ride some ramps and then talk some more. Catch ya later!

P.R.A.Y.

Leader: **Praise—Celebrate your relationship with Christ.**

All: Thank You, Jesus for being my Lord and Savior.

Leader: **Repent—Think about where you have fallen short in thought, word and deed. Then, with a genuine heart, ask for and accept His forgiveness and cleansing.**

All: Thank You, Lord, for Your forgiveness. Cleanse my heart, and make me the kind of person You want me to be.

Leader: **Ask—Go to the Savior for help. He is eager to meet your needs!**

All: Lord, help me with my problems. Give me the strength, wisdom and courage to face them.

Leader: **Yield—Submit to Christ, understanding that He knows what is best for you.**

All: Lord God, I submit my life to You. Call the shots and lead me.

Leader: **Amen.**

A Colorful Reminder

Green—Growth

We can now begin a new life in Christ! We can grow in His love, peace, strength and knowledge. A great adventure awaits when we let Jesus guide each step we take.

But grow in the grace and knowledge of our Lord and Savior Jesus Christ. To him be glory both now and forever! Amen.
2 Peter 3:18

Gold—Eternal Life

We have the promise of eternal life with Him and crowns of righteousness in heaven.

I write these things to you who believe in the name of the Son of God so that you may know that you have eternal life.
1 John 5:13

White—A Life Cleansed from Sin

We must accept God's gift of grace; we must also trust Jesus to be our Savior and to forgive us of our sins.

Yet to all who received him, to those who believed in his name, he gave the right to become children of God.
John 1:12

Red—Christ's Blood

Jesus Christ died and rose again so that our sins could be forgiven.

For Christ died for sins once for all, the righteous for the unrighteous, to bring you to God.
1 Peter 3:18

Black—Sin

Sin keeps us from having a personal relationship with God.

For all have sinned and fall short of the glory of God.
Romans 3:23

Teach Us to P.R.A.Y.
(Adults 18 and Up)

How to Use the Teach Us to P.R.A.Y. Adult Study

Prayer is such a prominent theme in the Christian's life, and yet it is a subject that many of us are unfamiliar with on a personal level. We love to talk about prayer, teach about prayer and pretend that we do a lot of praying, but the truth is we often come up short in the doing.

These sessions are intended to do one thing: to motivate people to pray. If you desire to help guide those you teach to the throne of grace, this study is for you. The lessons are Bible based and God focused. In exploring together, we hope that you and your students will discover the phenomenal joy and exciting power of prayer.

The six lessons are designed to build one upon another, escorting us from who God is through an understanding of the whys and hows of prayer and, finally, into the power of praying together. The lessons are simple, clear, interactive, spiritual and relevant. At the end of each chapter is a Portrait of Prayer, an incident from Scripture that illustrates how men and women accessed the promises of the creator by calling out to Him and the effects of their crying out.

The Sessions

Introduction
A brief introductory paragraph the teacher or a student can read aloud that helps to define what the lesson will encompass. You may also read the Key Verse at this time. Remember to open in prayer.

Object Lessons
Sometimes appearing before the Heartbeat section and other times after, the simple object lessons are designed to illustrate the points and provoke thought and discussion. Please read the next week's Preparation section each week to make sure you have the materials on hand or to give you time to talk to those who will help you with an illustration.

Heartbeat
The main body of the lesson encompasses one or more key points.

Reflection
A concluding paragraph provides food for thought to help solidify the truths taught in the lesson.

Take Time
An application suggestion gives students a simple activity to do in the coming week to reinforce the lesson.

Student Handouts

Some of the sessions ask students to write down intentions, prayers and other key points. This is where the student handouts are a valuable resource for students to take notes, answer questions and write down prayers.

The purpose of the Portrait of Prayer handouts is to encourage students to take a portion of the lesson home to meditate upon and apply the lessons during the week.

For Session Four, you'll need to order enough P.R.A.Y. bracelets for the entire class, plus extras for students to give to friends or family as reminders to pray. You can order these directly from the National Day of Prayer Task Force at 800-444-8828.

NOTE

Who Is God and Why Does He Want to Talk to Me?

Prayer is the most ancient, most universal and most intense expression of the religious instinct. Prayer is indeed the Christian's vital breath and native air. —J. Oswald Sanders

Goal of This Session

To establish that God—Jehovah, the Creator—has determined to have a relationship with those who call upon Him.

Key Verse

"Do you not know? Have you not heard? The LORD is the everlasting God, the Creator of the ends of the earth. He will not grow tired or weary, and his understanding no one can fathom." Isaiah 40:28

Biblical Basis

Genesis 16:7-13; 28:10-17; Exodus 3:1-6; Leviticus 11:44; Deuteronomy 4:32-40; 1 Chronicles 16:11,12; 2 Chronicles 7:14; Job 42:5; Psalms 139:7,8; 141:2; 145:18; Proverbs 3:5,6; Isaiah 35:8; 40:28-31; Matthew 5:44; 6:5; 11:25,26; 26:41; Mark 9:29; Luke 3:21; 5:16; 6:12; 9:18,28; 11:1; 12:7; John 14:16,17; 17; Acts 1:8; 2:42,47; 10:9-23; Romans 8:28,38,39; 12:12; Ephesians 6:18; Philippians 4:6,7; Colossians 3:12, 4:2; 1 Thessalonians 5:17; 1 Timothy 2:1,2; 4:8; Hebrews 4:15,16; 1 Peter 1:14,15; 5:5-7; James 4:6,7; 5:13-16; Revelation 1:8; 3:20; 5:2-8

Materials and Preparation

- Make copies of this session's student handouts (pp. 133-139).
- Have a white board and dry-erase markers, extra Bibles and pens or pencils available.
- Purchase a 30-foot long rope. You will also need a tape measure and three permanent felt-tip pens (green, red and black) with which to mark the rope.

Prepare the rope by drawing a large green dot in the middle of the rope. Twenty inches to the right of the green dot, place a red dot. Ten inches farther to the right, place two black lines, one inch apart.

125

Introduction

- Distribute the session handouts.
- Ask a volunteer to read the following information from the introduction of this session's student handouts:

> His words pierced the darkness like a mighty thunderclap rolling over and covering the abyss. With an angelic choir serenading this mysterious drama, a timeless God grasped the edges of infinity and gave the first invocation of life. With joyful and vigorous energy, God orchestrated this symphony of creativity with His voice. With unrestrained and unimaginable power and authority, He shaped and formed our world and universe, one divine word at a time.
>
> "Let there be light. Let there be sky. Stars begin your trek of light. Moon commence your orbit. Oceans burst forth, but here are your limits. Mountains raise up. Valleys sink low."
>
> Day after day, He spoke the underwater world, gravity and the animal kingdom into existence and harmony. Then on the sixth day, with His own hands He took dust, formed man and breathed into him life and essence.
>
> The living Word permeated the soul of man, and God said, "Speak with Me, call unto Me, seek My face."
>
> His desire has never changed. Just as Adam heard His voice riding on the breeze of the day, it still calls to us today, "I long for the pleasure of your company. Won't you join Me?"

Heartbeat

I. Who Is This God to Whom We Pray?

DISCUSS   What do you know about God?

Explain: **Throughout the history of God's dealings with man, He has gone to great lengths to reveal Himself. Yet He leaves a veil for each one of us to work past and pray through before we can have our personal glimpse and intimate knowledge of our creator. Prayer takes us by the hand and leads us through the boundaries of our finite limitations, guiding us into the territory and dimension of the holy. Prayer has many dimensions, but its main purpose is to take us to a place of discovery of Him.**

- Ask a student to read aloud Deuteronomy 4:32-40. This is a very dramatic passage, so choose a student who can read fluently and with feeling.

Continue: **Let's retrace the steps of those who have walked before us and encountered God through prayer. What do their meetings with God reveal to us?**

A. God Is Holy.

1. **Communion with God is holy ground.**

    Moses meets his Maker. Read Exodus 3:1-6; then explain: There were just some sheep and some ordinary bushes. Suddenly the commonplace was made extraordinary. Flames of fire burst from a bush. Having Moses' complete attention, God spoke. "Take off your sandals, for the place where you are standing is holy ground" (v. 5).

    Meeting with God is a sacred moment to be honored. Consequently, our times of prayer and communion are to be respected and held with reverence.

    The Lord can take the mundane moments of our lives and ignite them with the spectacular if we will only recognize who we are talking to and the unfathomable resource we connect to when we link our hearts with God's. The place of prayer is holy ground where our lives take a new direction, passion and hope. If your prayers have begun to feel common, it's time to petition your creator to show you His holiness.

What does "holy" mean? Can any of you describe a holy moment from your life?

DISCUSS

---

2. **"Holy" is a word that describes God's character.**

- Ask volunteers to read the following verses and discuss what each verse says about holiness:
  - **Leviticus 11:44** (absolutely pure and clean)
  - **Isaiah 35:8** (incorruptible)
  - **1 Peter 1:14,15** (separate from and intolerant of sin)

3. **You know you are on holy ground when you don't want to leave His presence.**

- Invite students to write a simple prayer of praise on their handouts. Ask them to suggest some descriptive words, such as "awesome," "majestic," "splendid," "excellent," "sublime," "exalted," "holy," "righteous," and write them on a white board or overhead transparency. If they are comfortable with the idea, have a few of them read their prayers aloud.

B. God Is Everywhere—Omnipresent.

1. Strength in prayer comes from knowing He is near.
   a. Psalm 145:18: "The LORD is near to all who call on him."
   b. Genesis 28:10-17: Jacob discovers the nearness of God. Jacob, weary from the day's journey, laid his head on the stone he had chosen for a pillow. Sleep came and with it a visitation. There, at the top of the angelic ladder, stood the Lord. Awakening from the dream, Jacob exclaimed, "Surely the LORD is in this place, and I was not aware of it . . . How awesome is this place" (vv. 16,17).

2. God is everywhere, all at once.
   Psalm 139:7,8: "Where can I go from your Spirit? Where can I flee from your presence? If I go up to the heavens, you are there; if I make my bed in the depths, you are there." Because He is near to someone else, does not take Him away from you. Often when we pray, we don't realize that God is near or that He is really listening. Therefore, our prayers are weak.

• Have students write "true" or "false" on their handouts beside each of the following statements:
   • Sometimes I go weeks without praying.
   • Our church services bore me.
   • God often seems distant to me.
   • My interest in my faith is equal to other interests in my life: my family, sports, my job, etc.

   Explain: God is always near—we are the ones who fade in and out of our relationship with Him. If you answered true to even one of the above statements, perhaps you need to ask yourself these questions:
   • *Is God the most important person in my life, or am I allowing other pursuits to push Him out of my life?*
   • *Is church really boring, or am I not really very faithful?*
   • *When I'm at church, am I just too tired to participate?*
   • *Do I truly expect God to speak to me when I pray, or am I just going through the motions?*

C. God Is Outside of Time.

1. God moves without limits, beyond time's grasp.
   Revelation 1:8: "'I am the Alpha and the Omega,' says the Lord God, who is, and who was, and who is to come, the Almighty.'"

OBJECT LESSON

Using the rope you have marked with the colored dots and lines, have two volunteers hold the rope, one at each end. You grasp the rope in the middle.

Explain: **The green dot symbolizes creation; the red dot stands for Christ's sacrifice on the cross. The black lines symbolize our entire lives. Since God lives outside of time and space, a thousand years could be like a moment.**

God is not subject to the limits of time. This means that He can prepare upcoming circumstances according to our prayers (examples: providing future job opportunities; preparing godly mates for our children). In addition, since God is beyond time, the death and resurrection of Christ is sufficient to atone for our sins, even though we weren't even born at the time of our Lord's sacrifice.

When we make requests to Him, when it seems the answer takes forever or when we don't get the answer we hoped for, God takes the long view. His perspective is eternal. His answers take our future and our best interests into account.

D. God Is All-Knowing—Omniscient.

1.   He is the beginning and the end of all understanding.
     Hagar's encounter with *El Roi*, "You are the God who sees," is described in Genesis 16:7-13. Hagar thought she was alone, that nobody cared and no one understood. Rejected and broken, pregnant with nowhere to live, she sat beside the spring mourning the collapse of her world. That is when God came beside her and introduced Himself as the omniscient One, the One who knows and understands everything.

     There is no problem that we have and no burden that we bear that God doesn't know about. His intention for us is that we would cast our cares upon Him.

2.   There is nothing God does not know.
     a.   God knew us when we were in our mother's womb.
          Jeremiah 1:5: "Before I formed you in the womb I knew you, before you were born I set you apart."
     b.   He knows the number of hairs on our head.
          Luke 12:7: "Indeed, the very hairs of your head are all numbered."

E. God Has Many Other Attributes.

1.   Immutable
     God does not change.
2.   Omnipotent
     God is all-powerful.
3.   Eternal
     God has no beginning and no end.
4.   Immanent
     God is active in His creation.

II. Why Does God Want To Talk To Me?

A. God Desires to Reveal Himself to You.

In the book of Revelation, God allows us to step into eternity and get a glimpse into His throne room. The apostle John had been taken in the Spirit into the place of God's habitation.

1. "And I saw a mighty angel proclaiming in a loud voice, 'Who is worthy to break the seals and open the scroll?' . . . I wept and wept because no one was found who was worthy to open the scroll or look inside. Then one of the elders said to me, 'Do not weep! See, the Lion of the tribe of Judah, the Root of David, has triumphed. He is able to open the scroll and its seven seals.' Then I saw a Lamb, looking as if it had been slain, standing in the center of the throne. . . . He came and took the scroll from the right hand of him who sat on the throne. And when he had taken it, the four living creatures and the twenty-four elders fell down before the Lamb. Each one had a harp, and they were holding golden bowls full of incense, which are the prayers of the saints" (Revelation 5:2-8).

This passage beautifully portrays how precious our prayers are in the sight of God. They are sweet smelling incense in His presence. When our praise and adoration for Him take wing, they are forever lifted up before Him. The prayers of those whom He has redeemed are continually treasured.

2. "May my prayer be set before you like incense; may the lifting up of my hands be like the evening sacrifice" (Psalm 141:2).

DISCUSS

If God knows everything, and understands our every need and short-coming, why do we need to pray?

B. Why Pray?

1. God wants us to pray our problems into His realm where He will bless, restore, forgive, heal and meet our every need.

   "'For I know the plans I have for you,'" declares the LORD, "'plans to prosper you and not to harm you, plans to give you hope and a future. Then you will call upon me and come and pray to me, and I will listen to you. You will seek me and find me when you seek me with all your heart'" (Jeremiah 29:11-13).

2. There are numerous reasons why we should pray.

   In each of the following lists, share all of the references and give students time to write them down; then choose one verse in each list to read aloud. Encourage students to take their lists home and read through each verse, underlining verses in their Bibles as they go.

   a. We are instructed in the Bible to pray.

      Matthew 5:44; Matthew 6:5; Romans 12:12; 1 Thessalonians 5:17; James 5:16

   b. We should follow Jesus' example and pray regularly.

      Matthew 11:25,26; Luke 3:21; Luke 5:16; Luke 6:12; Luke 9:18,28; Luke 11:1; John 17

   c. Prayer is how we communicate with, worship and praise God.

      Philippians 4:6; 1 Thessalonians 5:17

   d. Through prayer, God allows us to participate in His works.

Prayer can heal nations and grant us strength to endure trials, and it plays a part in bringing others to faith in Christ.

2 Chronicles 7:14; Isaiah 40:29-31; Hebrews 4:15,16

e. Prayer gives us power over evil.

Physical strength and power are of no use in the spiritual realm; even the physically weak can be strong in prayer.

Matthew 26:41; Mark 9:29; 1 Timothy 4:8; James 4:7

f. Prayer is always available to us.

Nothing can keep a believer from coming before God. Nations may condemn and forbid God's Word, but there are no barriers to prayer.

Psalm 139:7; Romans 8:38,39

g. Prayer keeps us humble before God.

Through prayer we realize that God is in control and we can do nothing apart from Him.

Jeremiah 32:17; John 15:5; Romans 8:28; Colossians 3:12; James 4:6,7; 1 Peter 5:5-7

h. Prayer grants us the privilege of experiencing God.

John 14:16,17; Acts 1:8; 10:9-23

i. Answered prayer has the potential to be an incredible witness to unbelievers.

Skeptics will always have criticisms and doubts regarding answered prayer, but some will see the power of God at work and, as a result, may be drawn to Christ.

Acts 2:42,47; James 5:16

j. Prayer strengthens the bonds among believers.

Scripture instructs us to pray for and confess our sins to one another. Through this, we learn empathy and understand the needs of others.

Ephesians 6:18; Colossians 4:2; 1 Timothy 2:1,2; James 5:13-16

k. Prayer succeeds where other means have failed.

Prayer is not be a last resort, but it can often make a difference where other methods have failed.

1 Chronicles 16:11,12; Proverbs 3:5,6; Philippians 4:6,7; James 5:15,16

What does God think of you? Does our perception of what God thinks of us affect how we pray? Does it affect how we live?   **_DISCUSS_**

Reflection

The call to prayer has never changed. From the opening of Genesis to Revelation, God is calling us to prayer. He used judges and prophets to plead with us to seek Him. Even in our own day, He continues to speak to us through His Son: "Here I am! I stand at the door and knock" (Revelation 3:20). Won't you let Him in?

The King of kings requests the pleasure of your company!

Take Time

Encourage students with the following: **Wake up each morning with a prayer of praise to God. Find and write down a favorite praise-oriented Scripture passage. Place it on your bathroom mirror, at your desk at work or where you will see it often. Read it out loud several times a day.**

Closing

Invite students to pray silently, thanking God for being just a prayer away.

Who Is God and Why Does He Want to Talk to Me?

Prayer is the most ancient, most universal and most intense expression of the religious instinct. Prayer is indeed the Christian's vital breath and native air. —J. Oswald Sanders

Goal of This Session

To establish that God—Jehovah, the Creator—has determined to have a relationship with those who call upon Him.

Key Verse

"Do you not know? Have you not heard? The LORD is the everlasting God, the Creator of the ends of the earth. He will not grow tired or weary, and his understanding no one can fathom." Isaiah 40:28

Biblical Basis

Genesis 16:7-13; 28:10-17; Exodus 3:1-6; Leviticus 11:44; Deuteronomy 4:32-40; 1 Chronicles 16:11,12; 2 Chronicles 7:14; Job 42:5; Psalms 139:7,8; 141:2; 145:18; Proverbs 3:5,6; Isaiah 35:8; 40:28-31; Matthew 5:44; 6:5; 11:25,26; 26:41; Mark 9:29; Luke 3:21; 5:16; 6:12; 9:18,28; 11:1; 12:7; John 14:16,17; 17; Acts 1:8; 2:42,47; 10:9-23; Romans 8:28,38,39; 12:12; Ephesians 6:18; Philippians 4:6,7; Colossians 3:12, 4:2; 1 Thessalonians 5:17; 1 Timothy 2:1,2; 4:8; Hebrews 4:15,16; 1 Peter 1:14,15; 5:5-7; James 4:6,7; 5:13-16; Revelation 1:8; 3:20; 5:2-8

Introduction

His words pierced the darkness like a mighty thunderclap rolling over and covering the abyss. With an angelic choir serenading this mysterious drama, a timeless God grasped the edges of infinity stand gave the first invocation of life. With joyful and vigorous energy, God orchestrated this symphony of creativity with His voice. With unrestrained and unimaginable power and authority, He shaped and formed our world and universe, one divine word at a time.

"Let there be light. Let there be sky. Stars begin your trek of light. Moon commence your orbit. Oceans burst forth, but here are your limits. Mountains raise up. Valleys sink low."

Day after day, He spoke the underwater world, gravity and the animal kingdom into existence and harmony. Then on the sixth day, with His own hands He took dust, formed man and breathed into him life and essence.

The living Word permeated the soul of man, and God said, "Speak with Me, call unto Me, seek My face."

His desire has never changed. Just as Adam heard His voice riding on the breeze of the day, it still calls to us today, "I long for the pleasure of your company. Won't you join Me?"

Heartbeat

I. Who Is This God to Whom We Pray?

A. God Is Holy.

1. **Communion with God is holy ground.**

   Moses meets his maker in Exodus 3:1-6.

2. **"Holy" is a word that describes God's character. What do the following verses say about God's holy character?**

   a. Leviticus 11:44

   b. Isaiah 35:8

   c. 1 Peter 1:14,15

3. You know you are on holy ground when you don't want to leave His presence.

Write a simple prayer of praise.

B. God Is Everywhere—Omnipresent.

1. Strength in prayer comes from knowing He is near.

   a. Genesis 28:10-17

   b. Psalm 145:18

2. God is everywhere, all at once.

   Psalm 139:7,8

Write "true" or "false" next to each of the following statements:

_____ 1.   Sometimes I go weeks without praying.

_____ 2.   Our church services bore me.

_____ 3.   God often seems distant to me.

_____ 4.   My interest in my faith is equal to other interests
               in my life: my family, sports, my job, etc.

Questions to ask yourself:
- *Is God the most important person in my life, or am I allowing other pursuits to push Him out of my life?*
- *Is church really boring, or am I not really very faithful?*
- *When I'm there, am I just too tired to participate?*
- *Do I truly expect God to speak to me when I pray, or am I just going through the motions?*

C. God Is Outside of Time.
Revelation 1:8

D. God Is All-Knowing—Omniscient.
1. He is the beginning and the end of all understanding.
   Genesis 16:7-13—*El Roi*

2. There is nothing God does not know.
   a. Jeremiah 1:5

   b. Luke 12:7

E. God Has Many Other Attributes.
1. Immutable

2. Omnipotent

3. Eternal

4. Immanent

II. Why Does God Want to Talk to Me?

A. God Desires to Reveal Himself to You.
Revelation 5:2-8

Psalm 141:2

B. Why Pray?
Jeremiah 29:11-13

a. We are instructed in the Bible to pray.

b. We should follow Jesus' example and pray regularly.

c. Prayer is how we communicate with, worship and praise God.

d. Through prayer, God allows us to participate in His works.

e. Prayer gives us power over evil.

f. Prayer is always available to us.

g. Prayer keeps us humble before God.

h. Prayer grants us the privilege of experiencing God.

i. Answered prayer has the potential to be an incredible witness to unbelievers.

j. Prayer strengthens the bonds among believers.

k. Prayer succeeds where other means have failed.

Reflection

The call to prayer has never changed. From the opening of Genesis to Revelation, God is calling us to prayer. He used judges and prophets to plead with us to seek Him. Even in our own day, He continues to speak to us through His Son: "Here I am! I stand at the door and knock" (Revelation 3:20). Won't you let Him in?

The King of kings requests the pleasure of your company!

Take Time

Wake up each morning with a prayer of praise to God. Find and write down a favorite praise Scripture passage and place it on your bathroom mirror, at your desk at work or where you will see it often. Read it out loud several times a day. Here are some suggestions:

- Psalm 9:1,2
- Psalm 44:6-8
- Psalm 84:10-12
- Romans 11:33-36
- Revelation 5:12,13

Portrait of Prayer
QUIT RAMBLING AND LISTEN!
(JOB)

When God says you don't know what you're talking about, it's best to quit rambling.

Job, brokenhearted and bruised with sores and sickness, had long debated with his friends concerning their concept of God and His motives.

"Sickness is punishment for sin, right? Well, then, Job, you must have sinned somewhere down the line! God does not punish without reason. What's going on in your life Job that you haven't told us about?" proclaimed his friends.

On and on they went declaring God's motives, purposes and reasons. Eloquently, they misjudged God. Self-righteously, they condemned Job. Confused, Job defended himself. Sadly, they were all wrong.

God finally interrupted Job and invited him into His world. "With all your knowledge, tell Me . . . where were you when I plotted out the dimensions of the earth? Did you invent the lightning? Or tell the snowstorm how to blanket the tundra?"

After the "tell Me," God cut through all the callused, ill-designed preconceptions Job had of Him and set Job on an odyssey of discovery of who He was. Wrong impressions dissipated and prepared the way for the birth of a new understanding of the creator.

When God finished His inquisition, Job uttered his wonder by proclaiming, "My ears had heard of you but now my eyes have seen you" (Job 42:5).

O, that we would pursue the prayer of discovery! God calls us to seek Him, seek His face, with no other motive than to become better acquainted, more intimate with Him.

In prayer we blast through the veil of our inhibited lives and soar into the realm where God is active and energetic on our behalf. Prayer is more than a religious formality. It is communing with the Most High, providing opportunity to discover the treasures of knowing Him.

1. How might my actions and prayers demonstrate the mistaken attitude that I know more than God?

2. In what ways might I be judging God and His actions?

3. How can I demonstrate a willingness to allow God to break down my preconceptions of His character?

4. How can I make my prayers more than a formal routine and truly commune with the Most High God, discovering the treasures of knowing Him?

Can My Prayers Really Make a Difference?

The devil is not terribly frightened of our human efforts and credentials. But he knows his kingdom will be damaged when we begin to lift up our hearts to God.—Jim Cymbala

Goals of This Session

- To show how our prayers function in the spiritual realm;
- To illustrate exactly how we can change the course of human events, even with the sovereignty of God at work.

Key Verse

"If my people, who are called by my name, will humble themselves and pray and seek my face and turn from their wicked ways, then will I hear from heaven and will forgive their sin and will heal their land." 2 Chronicles 7:14

Biblical Basis

Genesis 18:16-33; Exodus 32:9-14; Leviticus 11:45; Deuteronomy 4:7; 2 Chronicles 7:14; 30:9; Psalms 7:11; 85:10; 136; 145:17; Isaiah 13:11; 55:6,7; Ezekiel 22:30; Malachi 3:6; Ephesians 1:18—2:6; James 2:13; 1 John 4:8

Materials and Preparation

- Make copies of this session's student handouts (pp. 147-152).
- Have a white board and dry-erase markers, extra Bibles and pens or pencils available.
- Gather several small common tools (hammer, artist's brush, ink pen, frying pan or other kitchen tool, cloth tape measure, etc). Before class, place them on a table at the front of the room.

Introduction

- Distribute the session handouts.
- Ask a volunteer to read the following information from the introduction of this session's student handouts:

> This is a powerful lesson. The very concept of whether or not our prayers really work—and why—demands explanation; and an exciting and clear answer is found in God's Word. Having learned a little about this amazing God we serve, we can now discover the incredible power of our involvement in the prayer process with Him.

OBJECT LESSON

Lay out the tools you have gathered. Briefly discuss what each tool is used for; then ask, **What do all of these tools have in common?** They are all used by different artists or craftsmen: carpenter, artist, writer, chef, seamstress or furniture maker, etc. Also, these tools have no value whatsoever until they are placed in the hands of a master craftsman or artist.

Explain: **In the same way, we interact with God through the process of prayer in order to make a difference in our life circumstances. (1) We cannot affect a change in our lives or in the lives and hearts of others without the supernatural assistance of the Holy Spirit—all of our talents and gifts are useless in the eternal realm without God's help. (2) We are God's tools with which He affects change. Prayer is the connection between a willing mankind and our powerful and willing God.**

Heartbeat

I. Our Authority

A. We Are Identified with Christ.

"And God raised us up with Christ and seated us with him in the heavenly realms in Christ Jesus" (Ephesians 2:6).

Read Ephesians 1:18—2:6; then explain: **Once we are made alive in Christ through salvation and "because of his great love for us" (Ephesians 2:4), we are brought into a place of authority on the earth. As children of God, we have authority in Christ, just as Christ has been given all power and dominion. He is the head; we are the Body. Therefore, we can boldly approach the throne of grace.**

II. God's Justice and Mercy

A. His Justice and Holiness Are Reconciled to His Mercy and Love.

Two of the most important attributes of God are His justice and His mercy. God's justice is based upon His holiness, righteousness, moral authority, truth and knowledge of all things. God is a just Judge whose anger rightly burns against human evil. He will ultimately overcome and punish all evil.

Yet another attribute of God is mercy. His mercy is His loving-kindness in action; it is His desire to share His goodness with people who freely want to love and worship Him. It is His mercy that allows Him to look squarely at human sin and not banish us to eternal separation from Him forever: He took the full measure of human sin upon Himself, sending His Son to be the Savior of the world when we did not even want to be saved.

God's justice and mercy might seem to be opposed to each other, yet they are reconciled at the Cross. Psalm 85:10 (NKJV) says, "Mercy and truth have met together; righteousness and peace have kissed."

B. His Moral Character Is Perfect.

1. The moral *character* of God is unchangeable. He cannot tolerate sin; He is holy; He judges unrighteousness; His holiness must vindicate it. Share the following verses:
   - Leviticus 11:45: "Therefore be holy, because I am holy."
   - Psalm 7:11: "God is a righteous judge."
   - Isaiah 13:11: "I will punish the world for its evil, the wicked for their sins. I will put an end to the arrogance of the haughty and will humble the pride of the ruthless."
   - Malachi 3:6: "I the LORD do not change."
2. When we sin, God's holiness and righteousness demand just payment. Our every action will be held in account.

C. He Is Merciful by Nature.

1. The nature of God is different!
   God's nature is love—patient, kind, full of mercy and grace.
   a. 2 Chronicles 30:9: "For the LORD your God is gracious and compassionate. He will not turn his face from you if you return to him."
   b. Ephesians 2:4: "But because of his great love for us, God, who is rich in mercy, made us alive with Christ even when we were dead in transgressions—it is by grace you have been saved."
   c. 1 John 4:8: "Whoever does not love does not know God, because God is love."
2. He is a merciful God—when we repent.
   When we repent, God's mercy wells up from an infinite fountain. How often have we deserved the justice of God because of our sins? The clouds of punishment have gathered on our horizon, only to have the wind of the Spirit blow them over us and pour them out

on His Son. This is the nature of God. What we deserved fell on the heart of our Savior.

D. Mercy Is the Key to Prayer.

1. Mercy Triumphs.

   If God's merciful nature can be touched, then "mercy triumphs over judgment" (James 2:13), because love and mercy are more powerful than judgment!

   > Ezekiel 22:30: "I looked for a man among them who would build up the wall and stand before me in the gap on behalf of the land so I would not have to destroy it, but I found none."

   > Whether it is for our own redemption or for the pardon of a city or a nation, God wants us to call out to Him. Prayer gives us the right to move the arm of God's omnipotence through His loving and merciful nature. The wonder and mystery of it all is that God has chosen, for reasons best known to Himself, to cooperate with our efforts—the efforts we expend in response to His loving commands. How else do we explain the workings of prayer in any area of our lives?

   > As C.S. Lewis wrote, "Can we believe that God ever really modifies His action in response to the suggestions of men? For infinite wisdom does not need telling what is best, and infinite goodness needs no urging to do it." ("The Efficacy of Prayer"[1])

2. Why pray at all?

   The answer is as simple as it is profound and awe inspiring: The Lord wants to involve us in the process. As Pascal said (quoted by Lewis in "The Efficacy of Prayer"), "God instituted prayer in order to lend to His creatures the dignity of causality." God in His infinite wisdom has chosen to grant us the honor of participating in His works!

E. Prayer Changes the Course of History.

Deuteronomy 4:7: "What other nation is so great as to have their gods near them the way the LORD our God is near us whenever we pray to him?"

1. Scripture records man's appealing to God's merciful nature on behalf of others, after God had already declared His judgment.

   a. Genesis 18:16-33: Abraham negotiated with God on behalf of Sodom and Gomorrah.

   Note that God acknowledged the authority He had given Abraham and asked Himself if He should inform Abraham of His plan to destroy the cities. Abraham was given a chance to ask for mercy. Notice that there was no arm-twisting here. God was eager to say yes.

DISCUSS   How might God have spared Sodom and Gomorrah if Abraham had asked Him to spare the cities for just four people? Do you think there is ever a point of no return with God? Why or why not?

---

b. Exodus 32:9-14: Moses pleaded with God on behalf of the Israelites after their drunken orgy.

They still paid dearly for their rebellion, but Moses' appeal to God kept Him from destroying the Israelites completely. Moses ran interference for the Israelites several times throughout their desert journey.

2. The only hope for our communities and our nation rests in God who wants to use His people, motivating them to pray and then answering those prayers.

What is the difference between showing mercy and being unwise in allowing evil influence?

DISCUSS

How is it possible to pray for mercy for our leaders if they are blatantly promoting evil in our country?

3. We can appeal to the nature of God to heal our land, even when His character says that judgment is called for. (See Key Verse 2 Chronicles 7:14.)

F. Prayer Can Change the Course of Your Life.

1. There is interplay between God's mercy and His holiness.
   a. Psalm 145:17: "The LORD is righteous in all his ways and loving toward all he has made."
   b. Isaiah 55:6,7: "Seek the LORD while he may be found; call on him while he is near. Let the wicked forsake his way and the evil man his thoughts. Let him turn to the LORD, and he will have mercy on him, and to our God, for He will freely pardon."
2. We, too, can find our circumstances changed by appealing to God's merciful nature when we pray sincerely.
   a. According to His will
   b. In humility
   c. With authority
3. The blood of Jesus Christ clears a path of mercy between God's judgment and our despair.

   The nature of divine love overrides certain death.

Reflection

Responsive Reading

End this lesson with a responsive reading of Psalm 136. This powerful passage perfectly illustrates the beautiful fusion of God's character and His nature, and how they relate to us. You can read the first line of each verse, and the class members will respond in unison with the last half, "His love endures forever."

We serve a yes God!

Take Time

Remind yourself as you pray that your prayers can move the heart of God. Pray every day for our nation's leaders, that God will give them mercy and wisdom and that He will turn the hearts of those who do not promote godliness.

Closing

Close in prayer.

Note

1.   C. S. Lewis, "The Efficacy of Prayer" quoted in *The World's Last Night and Other Essays* (New York: Harcourt, Brace, Jovanovich, 1960), n.p.

Can My Prayers Really Make a Difference?

The devil is not terribly frightened of our human efforts and credentials. But he knows his kingdom will be damaged when we begin to lift up our hearts to God.—Jim Cymbala

Goals of This Session

- To show how our prayers function in the spiritual realm;
- To illustrate exactly how we can change the course of human events, even with the sovereignty of God at work.

Key Verse

"If my people, who are called by my name, will humble themselves and pray and seek my face and turn from their wicked ways, then will I hear from heaven and will forgive their sin and will heal their land." 2 Chronicles 7:14

Biblical Basis

Genesis 18:16-33; Exodus 32:9-14; Leviticus 11:45; Deuteronomy 4:7; 2 Chronicles 7:14; 30:9; Psalms 7:11; 85:10; 136; 145:17; Isaiah 13:11; 55:6,7; Ezekiel 22:30; Malachi 3:6; Ephesians 1:18—2:6; James 2:13; 1 John 4:8

Introduction

This is a powerful lesson. The very concept of whether or not our prayers really work—and why—demands explanation; and an exciting and clear answer is in God's Word. Having learned a little about this amazing God we serve, we can now discover the incredible power of our involvement in the prayer process with Him.

I. Our Authority

A. We Are Identified with Christ.

Ephesians 1:18—2:6

"And God raised us up with Christ and seated us with him in the heavenly realms in Christ Jesus" (Ephesians 2:6).

II. God's Justice and Mercy

A. His Justice and Holiness Are Reconciled to His Mercy and Love.

B. His Moral Character Is Perfect.

1. The moral character of God is unchangeable.

    a. Leviticus 11:45

    b. Psalm 7:11

    c. Isaiah 13:11

    d. Malachi 3:6

2. When we sin, God's holiness and righteousness demand just payment.

C. He is Merciful by Nature.

1. The nature of God is different!
    His nature is love. Love is patient, kind and full of mercy and grace.

    a. 2 Chronicles 30:9

    b. Ephesians 2:4

    c. 1 John 4:8

2. He is a merciful God—when we repent.

D. Mercy Is the Key to Prayer.

1. If God's merciful nature can be touched, then "mercy triumphs over judgment" (James 2:13), because love and mercy are more powerful than judgment!

    Ezekiel 22:30

2. Why pray at all? The Lord wants to _____ us in the _____!

E. Prayer Changes the Course of History.

Deuteronomy 4:7

1. Scripture records man's appealing to God's merciful nature on behalf of others, after God had already declared His judgment.

   a. Genesis 18:16-33

   b. Exodus 32:9-14

2. The only hope for our communities and our nation rests in God who wants to use His people, motivating them to pray and then answering those prayers.

F. Prayer Can Change the Course of Your Life.

1. There is interplay between God's mercy and His holiness.

   a. Psalm 145:17

   b. Isaiah 55:6,7

2. We, too, can find our circumstances changed by appealing to God's merciful nature when we pray sincerely.

   a. According to His will

   b. In humility

   c. With authority

3. The blood of Jesus Christ clears a path of mercy between God's judgment and our despair. The nature of divine love overrides certain death.

Reflection

Psalm 136 responsive reading

We serve a yes *God!*

Take Time

Remind yourself as you pray that your prayers can move the heart of God.
Pray every day for our nation's leaders, that God will give them mercy and wisdom and that He will turn the hearts of those who do not promote godliness.

Meditate on the following verses this week:
- Genesis 18:20-33
- 2 Chronicles 7:14
- James 5:16

Portrait of Prayer

THE LONGEST DAY

(JOSHUA)

Hurling through space at more than 65,000 mph, intricately balanced by the gravity of the sun some 93 million miles away, the earth, weighing over 5,000 billion billion tons, suddenly stopped spinning. Subduing time and space, God placed His finger on the planet. Somebody had prayed and God was moving outside of nature, going as far as changing the length of a solar day to provide the answer to that prayer.

Under divine direction, Joshua and his men had marched all night in order to catch the enemy unaware. With God's help they were conquering their adversary in a grand display, but daylight began slipping away. Joshua knew that with the darkness, the five kings and their armies would slip away too.

Looking heavenward, Joshua let his voice be heard in the presence of God and his army. "Lord, let the sun stand still," he prayed.

One man, one voice. How much difference can a lone individual make? Bringing the world to a screeching halt is a sizable example! Physically, Joshua stood powerless that day. But he called on his creator who, in turn, did the unbelievable. For hours the planet paused in space while Joshua and his men finished their battle.

Let your prayers be rekindled with the understanding that you really can make a difference. When called upon in prayer, God will take the impossible situations of our lives and bring victory out of them. We know that God is vitally interested in the affairs of mankind and that there are no limits to the lengths He will go in order to help us.

Turn your eyes heavenward, call on God and watch Him turn your world around. You really can make a difference!

"The sun stopped in the middle of the sky and delayed going down about a full day. There has never been a day like it before it or since, a day when the LORD listened to a man. Surely the LORD was fighting for Israel!" (Joshua 10:13,14).

1. What seemingly insurmountable task am I facing?

2. Are my actions demonstrating a limitless faith in a limitless God? In what areas does my faith falter?

3. Is God leading or prodding me toward something of which I am afraid? How can I place my trust in Him and move forward in obedience?

Moving Your Prayer Life from the "Ought to" to the "Want To"

Wherever a careless, fleshly Christian suddenly pulls his life together, turns on himself and seeks the face of God in penitence and tears, you have the beginning of a personal revival.—A.W. Tozer

Goals of This Session

- To emphasize the essential need for self-discipline in establishing a daily, consistent prayer life;
- To help us understand God's exciting involvement in our day as we fill it with the aroma of prayer.

Key Verse

"No discipline seems pleasant at the time, but painful. Later on, however, it produces a harvest of righteousness and peace for those who have been trained by it. Therefore, strengthen your feeble arms and weak knees. 'Make level paths for your feet,' so that the lame may not be disabled, but rather healed." Hebrews 12:11,12

Biblical Basis

Psalms 23:2; 32:8; 37:47; 51:6; 55:17; 90:14; Matthew 6:6,33; 13:45,46; 23:27; Luke 10:38-42; Philippians 3:14,15; Hebrews 12:11,12; James 4:2; 1 John 2:15-17

Materials and Preparation

- Make copies of this session's student handouts (pp. 162-167).
- Have a white board and dry-erase markers, extra Bibles and pens or pencils available.
- Obtain an X ray from a dentist or doctor that shows a cavity, injury, tumor, etc.
- Ask a volunteer to share a brief anecdote about a trip or special event that turned disastrous or comical because of lack of preparation. Or prepare to share an experience of your own.
- Before class, make arrangements with several people to interrupt the class when you give them a certain signal. You could have someone come in with a message for you, arrange to have a cell phone ring, someone could have his or her beeper go off, someone could go into a fit of coughing, etc. Meet with them beforehand and tell them in which order you want them to interrupt. The interruptions will all be done consecutively near the end of the Heartbeat section.

Introduction

- Distribute the session handouts.
- Ask a volunteer to read the following information from the introduction of this session's student handouts:

> It seems as if our generation is the busiest, fastest-moving in history. Global communication, increased mobility and inexpensive access to almost every kind of goods and services have propelled many of us into a mind-set of frenzied activity. Do you feel tired and behind schedule often? So do the millions who have bought into the concept of *more*. Society's faster pace seems to require us to pack more into a day just to keep up. Naturally, our leap onto the fast track can often mean that our spiritual needs get bumped way down on the priority list.
>
> But the truly valuable things in life require a reach. Finding a pearl "of great value" (Matthew 13:45,46) means stepping off the track, cooling our heels and making time for the one thing that truly matters—time with the Lord.

Heartbeat

I. Why Do We Need to Discipline Ourselves to Pray?

Explain: **When we truly understand the phenomenal difference that a daily prayer life will bring, we will be motivated and excited to spend greater amounts of time with the Lord.**

A. Prayer Puts Our Day in God's Hands.

1. **Preparation through prayer is the key to overcoming obstacles.**
   Have you ever been in a situation where you were not in control and the situation was very uncomfortable? Were there things you could have done that would have put you more in the driver's seat? Did you regret your lack of preparation and foresight?
   > **Psalm 55:17: "Evening, morning and noon I cry out in distress, and he hears my voice."**

2. **Begin each day in prayer.**
   When we do not begin our day with a time of concentrated, fervent prayer, we are already at a disadvantage, because we have to depend on only our limited natural resources for anything that may happen that day. When we go before the Lord in the morning, committing our day to Him and praying for our families, our world and our personal circumstances, we are setting in motion heavenly assistance for every detail of that day.

Psalm 32:8: "I will instruct you and teach you in the way you should go; I will counsel you and watch over you."

Life has no guarantees. Each day holds the potential for incredible joy or profound agony. We all need a great deal of wisdom, strength, self-discipline and help from the Holy Spirit to face each day. Life is fragile, and we are all vulnerable. When we engage the principles of prayer, we access the unlimited resources of heaven to help, deliver, guide, heal, protect—whatever the need. God is there for us, if we but ask.

B. It's Time to Grow Up in God.
1. Daily communication is important.

   As physical beings, we must breathe, eat, sleep and exercise to grow and be healthy. But we are also deeply spiritual beings. We cannot grow or remain spiritually healthy without a daily, consistent prayer life.

   Psalm 51:6: "Surely you desire truth on the inner parts; you teach me wisdom in the inmost place."

DISCUSS

What happens to a marriage when there is a ceasing of close communication on a daily basis?

How does one maintain a close friendship with a friend who lives far away?

By the same token, how can we personally know God without daily, intimate contact with Him and His Word?

Can we hear from the Lord if we never dialogue with Him?

How can our minds and hearts be stimulated and receptive to His guidance and how can new and fresh ways to help and minister to others enter our hearts if the flow of His Spirit is cut off through lack of contact?

Display the X ray and explain: **This X ray shows a problem that is not evident to the naked eye.** Go into a little detail here about the specifics of the X ray.

Continue: Often Christians like to maintain the appearances of outward health and maturity that don't exist. We're very good at all the appropriate Christian language, activity and demeanor. But only God sees the inside. We may know how to look and sound like healthy Christians, but inside we are often weak, sick and vulnerable because we simply aren't communicating with God. Just as we can often hide physical problems from others, so our spiritual maturity is hidden away where no one can see it.

2. Self-control and self-discipline indicate maturity.
   a. As adults, we sometimes practice selective self-control. We can work late on a project at work, stay up with a sick baby, plow through paperwork to file a tax return or crawl up into a filthy attic to fix a phone line because these are normal have-to jobs that adults do. But tending to our spiritual side takes just as much discipline, and because we can't see the deterioration happening on the inside, we don't prioritize those critical needs. Jesus warned the religious leaders of His day several times.

      Matthew 23:27: "Woe to you, teachers of the law and Pharisees, you hypocrites! You are like whitewashed tombs, which look beautiful on the outside but on the inside are full of dead men's bones."
   b. Christ calls us to a higher dimension, a noble and blessed place of fullness and perfection in Him.

      Philippians 3:14,15: "I press on toward the goal to win the prize for which God has called me heavenward in Christ Jesus." The apostle, Paul wrote these words from a Roman prison, knowing fully that he might not leave the prison alive. He had already endured torture and beatings, yet he continued to humbly encourage his friends in the church at Philippi to continue growing in Christ. Nothing stood in the way of his determination to keep his relationship with the Lord strong, deep and full of power.

   Our circumstances do not diminish the need for determined and directed prayer.

II. Develop Self-Discipline in Prayer.

Is busyness in itself necessarily bad? Why or why not?

Explain: **Being busy is not a sin.** Read the story of Mary, Martha and Jesus in Luke 10:38-42; then continue: **Martha loved the Lord—she was just *way* too task oriented! This illustrates a mind-set that we can all easily slip into. The**

Lord spoke directly to Martha's stressed-out attitude by reminding her that time with Him was most important.

For many of us, prayer is a very difficult thing to do on a daily basis, but there are no shortcuts. The only means of reaching our desired destination of Christian maturity is through prayer.

DISCUSS

Let's name a few reasons that we have given ourselves this past week to put off praying. Get specific! If needed to start the discussion, here are some examples:

- Emergencies: The washing machine overflowed just as I began my devotions.
- Schedules: My boss asked me to come in early; I forgot I had carpool.
- Tyranny of the urgent: I had to give a lecture to 400 people at 10 A.M. and a computer virus ate my notes; my mother-in-law just called and she's coming to stay for a week—she'll be here in two hours.
- Really lame: I was too frazzled in the morning and too tired at night; the Lord doesn't want me to have a dirty house/neglect my friends/lose any sleep/leave His work undone.

The truth is, regardless of our many reasons—many of them valid—we basically just don't have enough "want to" and discipline to pray. But as we have learned, we can't afford not to pray! So where do we start? Let's look at six specific ways in which we can get a grip on self-discipline and embark on a fresh, new prayer life.

A. Decide What You Want.

Identify areas of need.

Psalm 37:4: "Delight yourself in the LORD and he will give you the desires of your heart." What do you want or need to see happen in your life? What is missing? Prayer begins with a felt need—anything that causes you emotional distress such as pain, sorrow, frustration, anger, etc. We have to identify the areas in our lives or the lives of others that need God's help and intervention. This provides a goal, a specific target to move toward—a place to begin.

- Have the students write down three or four targets that they want or need to pray for. This is for their eyes only.

B. Ask God for Self-Discipline.

Ask God to place the desire and discipline to pray into your heart.
James 4:2: "You do not have, because you do not ask God." Ask fervently, daily and constantly. Suggested prayer:

Lord, I know what I need to do, but I just can't get there. Please plant in my heart a new desire—a new hunger—for Your presence. Make me restless and uneasy when I do not pray each day, and clear my mind of all excuses and distractions that would hinder my commitment to pray.

Nothing is closer to the heart of God than communication with His children. He will answer your prayer for self-discipline!

C. Begin Small, but Be Consistent.

Psalm 90:14: "Satisfy us in the morning with your unfailing love, that we may sing for joy and be glad all our days."

Name 10 things that can be accomplished in 15 minutes. Some examples might be: drive across town, mow the lawn, fix a meal and bathe a wiggling baby.

DISCUSS

Even though it's a short period of time in our busy schedules, let's begin by committing to pray 15 minutes a day. In another session we will discuss some how-to guidelines for prayer. For now, God wants us to make the deliberate *choice* to commit our will to pray daily. Fifteen minutes is doable for anyone. But watch out: your appetite for prayer will grow quickly!

D. Set Up a Reward/Discipline System.

Matthew 6:33: "But seek first his kingdom and his righteousness, and all these things will be given to you as well."

"Work, work from early till late. In fact, I have so much to do that I shall spend the first three hours in prayer."—Martin Luther

Our personal prayer time should be the first on our list of priorities. Determine that *no other* important priority will be met that day until you have spent time with the Lord. This is a radical approach, to be sure, but stick with it. Self-discipline requires dying to our own desires. He will generously reward your prioritizing your time with Him. Once you've given Him your day, let Him take care of the details. You'll find you can't out-give God!

E. Find and/or Set Up a Personal Prayer Space.

Matthew 6:6: "But when you pray, go into your room, close the door and pray to your Father, who is unseen. Then your Father, who sees what is done in secret, will reward you."

• Share the following examples of setting up personal prayer space:

Jim commutes an hour one way to work each day. He made the decision three years ago to use that hour alone to meet with God, praying (with his eyes open, of course!) for his family, friends, work, church and world, and to meditate and listen to the Lord. He says that time is sacred to him and has radically changed his life.

Ruth has fixed up a corner of her guest room with a comfortable chair, candles and soft lighting. This is her prayer room. In a desk drawer in the room she keeps a stack of prayer requests that she has either written down or collected from various sources or that have been given to her. She says, "My Lord and I have some wonderful times together in this room."

Where is your personal prayer space? Designating a special, private spot to meet with God helps to reinforce our commitment and desire to pray daily. It can be an entire room (if you like to pace while you pray), a favorite chair, a closet, your car, the garden or a city rooftop! God isn't concerned about geography. Wherever it is, He'll meet you there.

- Have students jot down two or three possible personal prayer spaces that they can begin using this week.

F. Tune Out the World.

Let *nothing*, short of a true emergency, interrupt your time with the Lord.

Ask students to share unique places in which they have prayed or places that they have heard of others using for prayer. During the sharing, begin the interruption skit.

INTERRUPTION SKIT

Begin talking; then give a prearranged signal for the interruptions to begin. After each one, you will try to get started again, speak a few words or phrases and then the next interruption should start. Don't go too fast, so they will look like real interruptions. Arrange enough interruptions to get the students fairly annoyed. Finally, you can come clean and confess that the interruptions were arranged.

After the skit, explain: As you can see, having our lesson time constantly interrupted was really annoying! In the same way, God is saddened when we allow all kinds of inconsequential interruptions into our time with Him. When you are in an important meeting at work with the boss, you instruct the secretary to hold all calls—no interruptions. How much more important is our meeting with the King of kings!

Psalm 23:2: "He leads me beside quiet waters."

Psalm 37:7: "Be still before the LORD and wait patiently for him."

Reflection

Explain: We are under constant surveillance by the enemy, Satan. He never takes a day off, never gets too tired and is never distracted from his mission to destroy us. He's very serious and disciplined about his mission to destroy us and our effectiveness. If we don't pray, we have no power to defend ourselves or to defeat the enemy.

Likewise, the busyness of life can become an enemy. Are we concentrating our time and efforts on this world, rather than on our true heavenly inheritance? Only when we work in partnership with God Himself can we live, grow and overcome. Read 1 John 2:15-17.

No prayer, no power. Much prayer, much power!

Take Time

Explain: **Begin each day the perfect way. Commit to spend at least 15 to 30 minutes each morning in prayer alone with the Lord and discover the difference it makes in your day! Remember: It takes 21 days to make or break a habit. Let's choose today to begin to make daily prayer a habit.**

Closing

Close in prayer.

DON'T FORGET TO ORDER P.R.A.Y. BRACELETS FOR THE NEXT SESSION IF YOU HAVEN'T ALREADY DONE SO.

Moving Your Prayer Life from the "Ought to" to the "Want To"

Wherever a careless, fleshly Christian suddenly pulls his life together, turns on himself and seeks the face of God in penitence and tears, you have the beginning of a personal revival.—A.W. Tozer

Goals of This Session

- To emphasize the essential need for self-discipline in establishing a daily, consistent prayer life;
- To help us understand God's exciting involvement in our day as we fill it with the aroma of prayer.

Key Verse

"No discipline seems pleasant at the time, but painful. Later on, however, it produces a harvest of righteousness and peace for those who have been trained by it. Therefore, strengthen your feeble arms and weak knees. 'Make level paths for your feet,' so that the lame may not be disabled, but rather healed." Hebrews 12:11,12

Biblical Basis

Psalms 23:2; 32:8; 37:47; 51:6; 55:17; 90:14; Matthew 6:6,33; 13:45,46; 23:27; Luke 10:38-42; Philippians 3:14,15; Hebrews 12:11,12; James 4:2; 1 John 2:15-17

Introduction

It seems as if our generation is the busiest, fastest-moving in history. Global communication, increased mobility and inexpensive access to almost every kind of goods and services have propelled many of us into a mind-set of frenzied activity. Do you feel tired and behind schedule often? So do the millions who have bought into the concept of more. Society's faster pace seems to require us to pack more into a day just to keep up. Naturally, our leap onto the fast track can often mean that our spiritual needs get bumped way down on the priority list.

But the truly valuable things in life require a reach. Finding a pearl "of great value" (Matthew 13:45,46) means stepping off the track, cooling our heels and making time for the one thing that truly matters—time with the Lord.

Heartbeat

I. Why Do We Need to Discipline Ourselves to Pray?

When we truly understand the phenomenal difference that a daily prayer life will bring, we will be motivated and excited to spend greater amounts of time with the Lord.

A. Prayer Puts Our Day in God's Hands.
1. Preparation through prayer is the key to overcoming obstacles.
   Psalm 55:17

2. Begin each day in prayer.
   Psalm 32:8

B. It's Time to Grow Up in God.
1. Daily communication is important.
   Psalm 51:6

2. Self-control and self-discipline indicate maturity.
   Matthew 23:27

Philippians 3:14,15

II. Develop Self-Discipline in Prayer.
Luke 10:38-42

List some specific ways in which you can get a grip on self-discipline and embark on a fresh, new prayer life.

A. Decide What You Want.
Psalm 37:4

Write down three or four targets that you want or need to pray for. This is for your eyes only.

B. Ask God for Self-Discipline.
James 4:2

Suggested prayer:
Lord, I know what I need to do, but I just can't get there. Please plant a new desire—a new hunger—for Your presence. Make me restless and uneasy when I do not pray each day, and clear my mind of all excuses and distractions that would hinder my commitment to pray. Amen.

C. Begin Small, but Be Consistent
Psalm 90:14

COMMIT

Commit to pray 15 minutes a day. But watch out: Your appetite for prayer will grow quickly!

D. Set Up a Reward/Discipline System.
Matthew 6:33

Our personal prayer time should be first on our list of priorities.

E. Find and/or Set Up a Personal Prayer Space.
Matthew 6:6

God isn't concerned about geography. Wherever it is, He'll meet you there. Write down two or three possible personal prayer spaces you can begin using this week.

F. Tune Out the World.
Let *nothing,* short of a true emergency, interrupt your time with the Lord.
Psalm 23:2: "He leads me beside quiet waters."

Psalm 37:7: "Be still before the Lord and wait patiently for him."

Reflection

We are under constant surveillance by the enemy, Satan. He never takes a day off, never gets too tired and is never distracted from his mission to destroy us. He's very serious and disciplined about his mission. If we don't pray, we have no power to defend ourselves or to defeat the enemy.

Likewise, the busyness of life can become an enemy. Are we concentrating our time and efforts on this world, rather than on our true heavenly inheritance? Only when we work in partnership with God Himself can we live, grow and overcome. Read 1 John 2:15-17.

No prayer, no power. Much prayer, much power!

Take Time

Begin each day the perfect way. Commit to spend at least 15 to 30 minutes each morning in prayer alone with the Lord and discover the difference it makes in your day! Remember: It takes 21 days to make or break a habit. Let's choose today to begin to make prayer a daily habit.

Read the following verses and write your thoughts in the space provided:

- Psalm 5:3

- Isaiah 55:6

- Mark 1:35

In his book *A Shepherd Looks at Psalm 23*, Phillip Keller observed:

Sheep, by habit, rise just before dawn and start to feed. Or if there is bright moonlight they will graze at night. The early hours are when the vegetation is drenched with dew, and sheep can keep fit on the amount of water taken in with their forage when they graze just before and after dawn. . . . In the Christian life it is of more than passing significance to observe that those who are often the most serene, most confident and able to cope with life's complexities are those who rise early each day to feed on God's Word. It is in the quiet, early hours of the morning that they are led beside the quiet, still waters where they imbibe the very life of Christ for the day. The biographies of the great men and women of God repeatedly point out how the secret of the success in their spiritual life was attributed to the "quiet time" of each morning. One comes away from these hours of meditation, reflection and communion with Christ refreshed in mind and spirit . . . the heart is quietly satisfied.[1]

Note

1. Phillip Keller, *A Shepherd Looks at Psalm 23* (Grand Rapids, MI: Zondervan Publishing House, 2000), n.p.

Portrait of Prayer

DO YOU HAVE THE "WANT TO"?
(1 SAMUEL 1—2)

Her heart launched the prayer, but the petition to God stuck in her throat. Hannah's desire for a child was so overwhelming that as she prayed her stomach seized and she couldn't breathe. Her sealed womb now caused her heart to burst. What her mouth uttered sounded more like a soul groan. Her lips found it impossible to verbalize this eruption coming from the core of her being.

Daily she prayed. Yearly she made the trek with her husband from the mountains of Ephraim to Shiloh in order to worship and to sacrifice. Monthly she found her prayers rejected. This year as she wept in the tabernacle, Eli the priest stood by the door and observed Hannah in her anguish. Seeing her lips moving but hearing no voice, he thought her to be drunk. "Put your wine away and sober up," he chided her.

Explaining to him that she was not drinking in but rather pouring out her heart before God, Eli realized his mistake and then he blessed her. In his blessing, Eli prophetically announced the petition she had cried out to God would be answered.

What God promised, He delivered! Out of the cry of a desperate woman's desire came the rosy-cheeked answer wrapped in a baby blanket. Hannah named her child Samuel, meaning "heard from God" or "because I have asked for him from the Lord."

The faithful, fervent prayer of this mother not only blessed her and her husband but also the whole nation of Israel. Samuel went on to become a judge of Israel and the man of God who anointed Saul and David to their roles as kings of Israel.

On her next pilgrimage to Shiloh after the birth of Samuel, Hannah and her husband dedicated him to the Lord. Listen in contrast how she begins her recorded prayer at the dedication, "My heart rejoices in the LORD!" (1 Samuel 2:1, *NKJV*).

There are times when the Lord allows us to demonstrate how much we want something before He answers. He checks to see how much "want to" we have in us. Some prayer is painful. But there is a payoff. "Weeping may endure for a night, but joy comes in the morning" (Psalm 30:5, *NKJV*)!

1. What is your deepest heartfelt petition of the Lord?

2. Have you passionately persevered in seeking God with your request?

3. In general, are you more like Eli or Hannah in this story? In what ways?

This, Then, Is How You Should Pray

We cannot learn about prayer except by praying. No philosophy has ever taught a soul to pray.—J. Oswald Sanders

Goals of This Session

- To provide a general framework within which we can pray on a daily basis, rather than aimlessly wander through our prayer time;
- To understand that only by actually practicing prayer will we truly develop the prayer life we desire.

Key Verse

"Devote yourselves to prayer, being watchful and thankful." Colossians 4:2

Biblical Basis

1 Samuel 13:114; 2 Samuel 12; Psalms 51:6,10-11; 65—66; 68:19; 100:4; 119:105; 139:1-24; Matthew 6:9-13; Luke 11:1; 19:1-9; John 10:27; 2 Corinthians 7:10; Ephesians 3:20,21; 6:18; Philippians 4:6; Colossians 4:2; Hebrews 4:16; James 4:3; 1 John 5:14,15; Revelation 3:20

Materials and Preparation

- Make copies of this session's student handouts (pp. 178-186).
- Have a white board and dry-erase markers, extra Bibles and pens or pencils available.
- Prepare for the 9-1-1 skit by asking someone ahead of time to pretend to be injured and in need of medical assistance. Decide beforehand where he or she will be located. The location needs to be a well-known spot in your community: a park, courthouse, lake, mall, airport, etc.
- Prepare two drinking glasses (one filthy and crusty, one clean). Fill both with ice and a clear beverage just before starting the session.

Introduction

- Distribute the session handouts.
- Ask a volunteer to read the following information from the introduction of this session's student handouts:

> Prayer is a very spiritual activity. Communication with God is intimate, dynamic and profoundly soul driven. At the same time, many people approach God as strangers, feeling awkward and ineffective, even during moments of crisis. The simple pattern in this lesson provides a framework for our prayers. It is an outline in which we can place all of those heart issues in an order that is biblical, spiritual and powerful. Only we, with God's help, can give our prayers meaning and power, but this outline will give direction to many who need help to develop a daily relationship with the Lord. It will also help many seasoned Christians develop more rounded and well-balanced prayer times.

Explain: **Before we discuss how to use the P.R.A.Y. pattern, we need to examine our attitude toward God as we enter our time of prayer. Let's take a look at the psalmist David, whose prayer life is a great example to follow.**

Heartbeat

I. Our Attitude Toward God As We Pray

Explain: **David—shepherd, warrior, king—was a man who knew the secret of true communication with God. What was that secret? Transparency. The book of Psalms is a tale of a heart laid bare, in triumph and despair, inviting, even begging, God to be involved in every moment. David's utter openness toward his Creator showed communion with Him on a level rarely seen elsewhere in Scripture. Even when David committed a terrible sin and was confronted by the prophet Nathan, he ran toward the Lord in repentance. God had finally found a man after His own heart.**

A. Be Honest.

1 Samuel 13:14: "The LORD has sought out a man after his own heart and appointed him leader of his people."

As we approach our heavenly Father in prayer, we must be prepared to be completely honest and open before Him. The four steps we'll be studying are a clear invitation for God to search the inner recesses of our hearts, since we can't make much progress unless we are willing to be absolutely truthful with ourselves and with Him.

Have the person you have chosen beforehand come to the front of the room. Explain that this person is in a well-known spot somewhere in your community, is injured and has called 9-1-1. The class members will be the 9-1-1 operators and must discover where the injured person is in fewer than 10 questions. The injured person is very weak and can only answer with a yes or no.

9-1-1 SKIT

How much good can the paramedics do for this person if they can't get to him or her?

DISCUSS

B. Hide Nothing.

Revelation 3:20: "Here I am! I stand at the door and knock."

We often try to withhold parts of ourselves from God. Of course, He knows where we are and all of our hidden thoughts, deeds and sins. However, He wants us to make every room, every corner and every closet within our hearts voluntarily available, so that He can help us, take care of us and lead us along life's journey.

Psalm 139:1-24 beautifully portrays David's transparency before God. "Search me, O God, and know my heart; test me and know my anxious thoughts" (v. 23).

II. The Power of P.R.A.Y.

Distribute the P.R.A.Y. bracelets and explain: **Praise—Repent—Ask—Yield** is used to describe a dynamic approach to prayer! The elements of these four prayer points are all found in Matthew 6:9-13, in the well-known Lord's Prayer. Jesus' instructions, "This, then, is how you should pray" indicated His firm desire that we know exactly how to call upon Him (v. 9). Note, too, that in a parallel passage found in Luke, Christ's followers were eager to learn how to pray: "Lord, teach us to pray, just as John taught his disciples" (Luke 11:1). The following phrases of the Lord's Prayer are taken from the *New King James Version*. (The rest of the verses are from the *NIV*.)

A. *P* = Praise

Matthew 6:9: "In this manner, therefore, pray: Our Father in heaven, hallowed be Your name."

Matthew 6:13: "For Yours is the kingdom and the power and the glory forever. Amen."

1. The Lord's Prayer begins and ends with praise!
    Psalm 100:4: "Enter his gates with thanksgiving and his courts with praise; give thanks to him and praise his name."
2. Praise accomplishes three important things.
    a. It reestablishes the relationship.
        In His presence we are vividly reminded that He is God, and we're not. As we glorify Him, He is established in our minds and hearts as Lord and master over not just the universe but

also over our lives. We are repositioned into a place of humility before Him—His workmanship, His children, His beloved. We are ushered into His presence, filled with awe and wonder at this God we serve. At the same time, we move from being self-centered with worry and distress to being reverently and peacefully God-centered.

b. It generates gratitude.

Psalm 68:19: "Praise be to the Lord, to God our Savior, who daily bears our burdens." Throughout the psalms, in verses like this, David interwove his praises with thankfulness and reminders of what God had done for him. The moment we begin to praise God, our hearts make it personal. We can't help but remember those blessings and miracles, large and small, that God has generously bestowed upon us.

- Have students write down three prayers God has recently answered. Take one or two minutes to allow the class members to silently give thanks for these answered prayers.

c. It builds faith.

- Read aloud one of the following psalms of praise: Psalm 65, 66 or 135; then explain:

This psalm reminds us of how magnificent God is and the wonderful things He has done. In praise and worship we remember just who it is we are talking to—God Almighty! Worship says, "Your prayers are being heard in the courts of eternity right now, and the Lord Himself is waiting to hear your petitions." We can now pray, knowing that the very God of the universe is inclining His ear toward us, eager to help.

This is an important point. Many times we say that we serve, believe in and trust in the Lord, but we don't treat Him like God when we pray. We often shrink Him down in our minds to where He is barely recognizable as the God of the ages portrayed in Scripture—the God we know that He truly is. Praise reverses this. As we praise, we are refilled with the knowledge of His power and glory. We have renewed faith that He can and will meet our needs—because, after all, He is God.

B. *R* = Repent

Matthew 6:12,13: "Forgive us our debts, as we forgive our debtors. And do not lead us into temptation, but deliver us from the evil one."

1. The Lord's Prayer recognizes the need to repent of our wrongdoing.

In addition, we are instructed to ask for God's help to keep away from future sin.

Bring out the two glasses you have previously prepared (one filthy, one clean.) Both should be filled with ice and a beverage. Offer both glasses to several class members. The dirty glass probably won't get any takers!

Most people are pretty careful about daily physical cleanliness. But we often try to drink from the pure water of the Spirit with vessels—hearts—that are clogged and crusty with ungodly activities and attitudes. Daily purification through repentance washes away the soil of life's journey.

2. Repentance has three important effects.
   a. It allows us to remain in God's presence.
      Psalm 51:10-11 (*NKJV*): "Create in me a clean heart, O God, and renew a steadfast spirit within me. Do not cast me from Your presence, and do not take Your Holy Spirit from me."

      God is holy; His character will not tolerate sin. God cannot communicate intimately with us, or bless and help us, if our hearts are unrepentant or if we allow sin to remain anywhere in our lives.

DISCUSS

Have students discuss in small groups several things that they may do during the course of a day that are in violation of God's Word. Examples: Losing one's temper, telling a white lie, an unforgiving attitude, gossip, laziness, nurturing impure thoughts, etc.

   b. It encourages honesty before God.
      Psalm 51:6: "Surely you desire truth in the inner parts; you teach me wisdom in the inmost place."

      Daily repentance gets us in the habit of openness before God. In addition, a daily housecleaning keeps us more aware of sin the next time we are tempted. We are more likely to recognize the temptation and resist if we have repented for that very thing earlier the same day.
   c. It allows healing to begin.
      When our bodies have an open wound, the first thing the physician will do is clean it to remove the possibility of infection and promote healing. Repentance removes old sins and attitudes and opens the way for the Holy Spirit to do a deep inner healing.
3. There are three components of repentance.
   a. We must recognize what we have done and that it is wrong.
      In 2 Samuel 12, Nathan the prophet confronted David about his adultery with Bathsheba and murder of her husband, Uriah. When Nathan is finished with the Lord's rebuke, David immediately admits his sin.
   b. We must be truly sorry for our sin and express the intent to turn away from it.
      2 Corinthians 7:10: "Godly sorrow brings repentance that leads

to salvation and leaves no regret." The Lord loves a tender, repentant heart. He is rich in mercy when we call upon Him in repentance!

    c. We must show the willingness to make amends.

       In Luke 19:1-9, the story of Zacchaeus, the tax collector, reminds us that when righting our wrongs is possible, the Lord expects us to do so. Zacchaeus proved how sorry he was by returning the money he had embezzled.

C. *A* = Ask

Matthew 6:11: "Give us today our daily bread."

1. The Lord's Prayer shows us an approachable God who wants us to come to Him with our needs! Of course, He already knows our needs, but in our asking we display a trust in and dependence upon Him which is essential to our spiritual well-being.

    1 John 5:14,15: "This is the confidence we have in approaching God: that if we ask anything according to his will, he hears us. And if we know that he hears us—whatever we ask—we know that we have what we asked of him."

2. There are four components of asking in prayer.

    a. Ask humbly.

       Philippians 4:6: "Do not be anxious about anything, but in everything, by prayer and petition, with thanksgiving, present your requests to God."

       Show reverence, respect and thanksgiving. Remember and acknowledge that you are talking to God Almighty.

    b. Ask boldly.

       Hebrews 4:16: "Let us then approach the throne of grace with confidence, so that we may receive mercy and find grace to help us in our time of need."

       Jesus consistently reminded us that we are His children and precious to Him. His death and resurrection cleared the way for us to enter His presence and go directly to Him with our needs.

    c. Ask realistically.

       James 4:3: "When you ask, you do not receive, because you ask with wrong motives, that you may spend what you get on your pleasures."

       We cannot ask God to manipulate, stretch or bend His Word and laws to fit our desires or circumstances. We should also use common sense when we talk with God. The Bible provides a straightforward, easy-to-understand design for our lives. No second-guessing of His Word is allowed.

• Ask volunteers to read the examples from the session handout titled "You Can't Manipulate God!" (p. 175). Discuss each as indicated.

You Can't Manipulate God!

Example One

Since the Bible speaks clearly against gossip, we shouldn't pray about whether or not we should repeat a bit of juicy news to a friend so they can "pray" for the person we are gossiping about. That's manipulation of the Word.

> **Have you been guilty of this or know others who might do this** (don't share names or ask for a show of hands, just let them think about it for a moment)? **How can we avoid the trap of using prayer to spread gossip?**

DISCUSS

Example Two

You want to enter a business venture that will keep you away from your family and out of church for long periods of time. You say you want to do this so that you can "bless" the church with the money. Nice try, but staying away from your family and not being faithful to church are clear violations of God's Word. No need to pray about it!

> **What should you do when a supervisor asks you to do this or risk losing your job? What do you do if your job requires you to work Sundays or takes you away from your family for lengths of time, such as is required of police officers, firefighters, nurses, doctors, professional athletes, etc.?**

DISCUSS

Example Three

A man who had frequented a donut shop every morning for years finally stopped going, because he had gained so much weight. After staying away for several weeks, he showed up at the counter one morning. The owner asked him what made him come back and he replied, "Well, I was driving by this morning and asked the Lord, 'If it is Your will for me to go in and have some donuts this morning, let there be an open parking space right in front of the shop.' Sure enough, on my tenth time around the parking lot, there it was!"

> **Can you think of similar, perhaps less obvious, examples of this? How can you avoid this pitfall?**

DISCUSS

    d. **Ask creatively.**
        Ephesians 3:20,21: "Now to him who is able to do immeasurably more than all we ask or imagine, according to his power that is at work within us, to him be glory in the church and in Christ Jesus throughout all generations, for ever and ever! Amen."

Pray with faith, expecting God to do amazing things! Be visionary and optimistic and ask God to display His power and glory in your life.

Ephesians 6:18: "And pray in the Spirit on all occasions with all kinds of prayers and requests. With this in mind, be alert and always keep on praying for all the saints."

D. *Y* = Yield

Matthew 6:10: "Your kingdom come. Your will be done on earth as it is in heaven."

1. The Lord's Prayer recognizes God's sovereignty.

This part of our prayer time is the peaceful part. In the final analysis, God is still on His throne in control, omniscient, omnipresent. Now is when we die to ourselves, our desires, our need to be in charge and give everything to Him. Prayer transforms our will into His will. We rest in Him, and we trust in His Word, His power and His love for us.

• Have students write down a prayer that includes just one thing in their lives that they are giving over completely to God.

2. There are two ways to yield.

a. Read the Word.

Psalm 119:105: "Your word is a lamp to my feet and a light for my path."

Keep your Bible close by as you pray. Search the Scriptures; meditate upon the words of life found there. Write them down in a prayer journal, if you keep one. Begin memorizing favorite verses.

b. Listen.

John 10:27: "My sheep listen to my voice; I know them, and they follow me."

The more time we spend with the Lord, the more familiar His voice will become. Quiet time spent in silent contemplation of God, allowing His Spirit to minister to us, brings us close to Him. Let God speak to your heart.

Reflection

Explain: God is watching us very closely. The Holy Spirit is also active around us at all times. He passionately pursues us, longing to hear from us and to commune with us. Pray with fervency and yearning toward God. Don't disrespect Him with casual, halfhearted prayers and empty words that go nowhere. Reach for God with your whole heart! And remember, everything that does or does not happen in our prayer lives has the potential to directly affect the rest of our lives.

The VERTICAL—our relationship with God—
directly affects
The HORIZONTAL—our relationship with others!

Take Time

Explain: Begin a brand new P.R.A.Y.-er life. Come to your heavenly Father with transparency and passion. Give Him honor, clean your heart's house, ask with confidence, and then give it all to Him. But be ready for life-changing things to happen!

Closing

Close in prayer.

This, Then, Is How You Should Pray

We cannot learn about prayer except by praying. No philosophy has ever taught a soul to pray.—J. Oswald Sanders

Goals of This Session

- To provide a general framework within which we can pray on a daily basis, rather than aimlessly wander through our prayer time;
- To understand that only by actually practicing prayer will we truly develop the prayer life we desire.

Key Verse

"Devote yourselves to prayer, being watchful and thankful." Colossians 4:2

Biblical Basis

1 Samuel 13:114; 2 Samuel 12; Psalms 51:6,10-11; 65—66; 68:19; 100:4; 119:105; 139:1-24; Matthew 6:9-13; Luke 11:1; 19:1-9; John 10:27; 2 Corinthians 7:10; Ephesians 3:20,21; 6:18; Philippians 4:6; Colossians 4:2; Hebrews 4:16; James 4:3; 1 John 5:14,15; Revelation 3:20

Introduction

Prayer is a very spiritual activity. Communication with God is intimate, dynamic and profoundly soul driven. At the same time, many people approach God as strangers, feeling awkward and ineffective, even during moments of crisis. The simple pattern in this lesson provides a framework for our prayers—an outline upon which we can place all of those heart issues in an order that is biblical, spiritual and powerful. Only we, with God's help, can give our prayers meaning and power, but this outline will give direction to many who need help to develop a daily relationship with the Lord. It will also help many seasoned Christians develop more rounded and well-balanced prayer times.

Heartbeat

I. Our Attitude Toward God As We Pray

David—shepherd, warrior, king—was a man who knew the secret of true communication with God. What was that secret? Transparency.

A. Be Honest.

1 Samuel 13:14

B. Hide Nothing.

Revelation 3:20

Psalm 139:1-24: "Search me, O God, and know my heart; test me and know my anxious thoughts" (v. 23).

II. The Power of P.R.A.Y.

Praise, Repent, Ask, Yield—a dynamic approach to prayer! The elements of these four prayer points are all found in Matthew 6:9-13, in the well-known Lord's Prayer. The following Lord's Prayer verses are taken from the *New King James Version*.

A. *P* = Praise

Matthew 6:9: "In this manner, therefore, pray: Our Father in heaven, hallowed be Your name."

Matthew 6:13: "For Yours is the kingdom and the power and the glory forever. Amen."

1. **The Lord's Prayer begins and ends with praise!**
    Psalm 100:4

2. **Praise accomplishes three important things.**
    a. It reestablishes the relationship.

    b. It generates gratitude.

        Psalm 68:19

        Describe three of your prayers that God has recently answered.

    c. It builds faith.

        Psalm 65

        Psalm 66

        Psalm 135

B. *R* = **Repent**

Matthew 6:12,13: "Forgive us our debts, as we forgive our debtors. And do not lead us into temptation, but deliver us from the evil one."

1. **The Lord's Prayer recognizes the need to repent of our wrongdoing. In addition, we are instructed to ask for God's help to keep away from future sin.**

2. Repentance has three important effects.

    a. It allows us to remain in God's presence.

        Psalm 51:10,11

        Write down several things you may do during the course of a day that are in violation of God's Word.

    b. It encourages honesty before God.

        Psalm 51:6

    c. It allows healing to begin.

3. **There are three components of repentance.**

    a. We must recognize what we have done and that it is wrong.

2 Samuel 12

b. We must be truly sorry for our sin and express the intent to turn away from it.

2 Corinthians 7:10

c. We must show the willingness to make amends.

Luke 19:1-9

C. *A* = **Ask**

Matthew 6:11: "Give us today our daily bread."

1. The Lord's Prayer shows us an approachable God, who wants us to come to Him with our needs!

1 John 5:14,15

2. There are four components of asking in prayer.
   a. Ask humbly.

Philippians 4:6

b. Ask boldly.

Hebrews 4:16

c. Ask realistically.

James 4:3

d. Ask creatively.

Ephesians 3:20,21; 6:18

D. *Y* = **Yield**
Matthew 6:10: "Your kingdom come. Your will be done on earth as it is in heaven."

1. **The Lord's Prayer recognizes God's sovereignty.**

Write down a prayer that includes just one thing in your life you are giving over completely to God.

2. **There are two ways to yield.**

    a. Read the Word.

         Psalm 119:105

    b. Listen.

         John 10:27

Reflection

God is watching us very closely. The Holy Spirit is also very active around us at all times. He passionately pursues us, longing to hear from us and to commune with us. Pray with fervency and yearning toward God. Don't disrespect Him with casual, half-hearted prayers and empty words that go nowhere. Reach for God with your whole heart! And remember: Everything that does or does not happen in our prayer lives has the potential to directly affect the rest of our lives.

The VERTICAL—our relationship with God—
directly affects
The HORIZONTAL—our relationship with others!

Take Time

Begin a brandnew P.R.A.Y.-er life. Come to your heavenly Father with transparency and passion. Give Him honor, clean your heart's house, ask with confidence, then give it all to Him. But be ready for life-changing things to happen!

Meditate on the following verses this week:

- Psalm 51:10-12
- Psalm 116
- Luke 9:28-36

You Can't Manipulate God!

Example One

Since the Bible speaks clearly against gossip, we shouldn't pray about whether or not we should repeat a bit of juicy news to a friend so they can "pray" for the person we are gossiping about. That's manipulation of the Word.

Example Two

You want to enter a business venture that will keep you away from your family and out of church for long periods of time. You say you want to do this so that you can "bless" the church with the money. Nice try, but staying away from your family and not being faithful to church are clear violations of God's Word. No need to pray about it!

Example Three

A man who had frequented a donut shop every morning for years finally stopped going, because he had gained so much weight. After staying away for several weeks, he showed up at the counter one morning. The owner asked him what made him come back and he replied, "Well, I was driving by this morning and asked the Lord, 'If it is Your will for me to go in and have some donuts this morning, let there be an open parking space right in front of the shop.' Sure enough, on my tenth time around the parking lot, there it was!"

Portrait of Prayer

A MOMENT ON THE MOUNTAIN

(LUKE 9:28-36; 22:39-46; MATTHEW 26:36-46)

"Peter, James, John, accompany Me up the mountain to pray." By special invitation these three had been invited to be witnesses to a spectacular moment in the ministry of Christ. Of course they didn't realize this. They just enjoyed going with Jesus to pray. The trek included wonderful views and being away from all the people and commotion, and the exercise was a nice bonus. At the top of the mountain, Jesus stopped and began to pray. They followed His example. Peter began his prayer, "Mighty God, Creator of heaven and Earth, I praise You today. Guide my prayers as I seek Your face. Show Yourself . . ." and off to sleep he went! Ditto for James and John. Something snapped them back to consciousness and when they looked for Jesus, they beheld Him being transfigured. His face was as bright as a flash of lightning, and He was talking with Moses and Elijah! The disciples were in awe of the glorious splendor they were witnessing. Suddenly a cloud enveloped them and they heard the very voice of God, "This is My Son, whom I have chosen; listen to Him."

A breathtaking moment, and to think they almost missed it because of sleep.

Later, these same three were taken by Jesus into the garden by special request again. Jesus asked them to pray with Him for He was deeply distressed, "Even to the point of death." Jesus walked a short distance away to pray, and when He came back over, the disciples were already fast asleep. He told them to "watch and pray," lest they be overwhelmed by temptation. He told them that their spirits were willing, but their flesh was the weak element. We know the rest of the story.

We are no different from the disciples. We agree that prayer is important. It is essential! But how often do we get caught sleeping? Wonderful moments can pass us by while our eyes are heavy and our minds dull. Let the words of Jesus be ours today. Let's "watch and pray."

1. How often do you fall asleep while praying?

2. Do you view prayer as exciting or boring? Why?

3. What can you do to remain more alert and diligent in prayer? List at least five things you can do to remain alert while praying.

Lord, Teach Us How to Really Pray

The greatest value in trouble comes to those who bow lowest before the throne.—E.M. Bounds

Goals of This Session

- To help us understand the three different levels of prayer, the differences among them and how each is important to our spiritual walk;
- To explore the deeper, more intense times of prayer: "praying in the Spirit," "praying through" and intercession.

Key Verses

"Arise, cry out in the night, as the watches of the night begin; pour out your heart like water in the presence of the Lord. Lift up your hands to him for the lives of your children, who faint from hunger at the head of every street." Lamentations 2:19

"Ask and it will be given to you; seek and you will find; knock and the door will be opened to you. For everyone who asks receives; he who seeks finds; and to him who knocks, the door will be opened." Matthew 7:7

Biblical Basis

Deuteronomy 26:7; 1 Samuel 1:10-16; 2 Samuel 24:24; Psalms 23; 50:15; 130:1,2; Isaiah 55:6; Jeremiah 33:3; Lamentations 2:19; Daniel 10:10-13; Matthew 7:7; Luke 8:43-48; 18:1-8; 22:39-44; Romans 8:26,27; Ephesians 6:18; Colossians 4:12; Hebrews 5:7

Materials and Preparation

* Make copies of this session's student handouts (pp. 194-200).
* Have a white board and dry-erase markers, extra Bibles and pens or pencils available.
* Gather the following items: a small glass of soda (Pepsi, Coke, etc.), half a lemon or a few lemon slices, a bottle of Tabasco sauce, a spoon, a glass or bottle of clean water and a blindfold. Before anyone arrives, place items on a table at the front of the room. Cover everything except the blindfold with a cloth so that the items can't be seen until you're ready to do the object lesson.

Introduction

- Distribute the session handouts.
- Ask a volunteer to read the following information from the introduction of this session's student handouts:

> God loves to communicate. In turn, He has designed it so that our health, hope and salvation lie in our determination to call upon Him. There is no other way! We simply can't live the Christian life without an active prayer life.

Heartbeat

I. Three Dimensions of Prayer

Explain: **God's most passionate desire is that we call upon Him. "Call out to Me and I'll answer," He promises over and over. When Jesus instructed us to ask, seek and knock, He wasn't only repeating the same instruction three times. He was teaching us about** *three specific levels* **of prayer. And each level of prayer is essential!**

OBJECT LESSON

Ask for an adventurous volunteer. As you blindfold him or her, explain that you are going to have him or her taste three different levels of intensity. Give him or her the following items in the order listed here: a sip of the soda, a taste of the lemon and a few drops of the Tabasco sauce on the spoon. The water is for after the taste test!

Ask the guinea pig—er, volunteer—to describe the experience (i.e., the sensation, the taste, etc.).

Explain: **The first taste is like the first level of prayer: It's sweet and lacks specific intensity. The second taste, the lemon, represents an out-of-the-ordinary experience—more compelling, more attention getting. The third taste, the Tabasco sauce, gets our attention! For most people, it's a very sharp, intense taste—not easily forgotten. In the same way, the Tabasco sauce represents the third level of prayer, which is urgent and focused. There are definite differences in the kinds of prayers we pray. As we understand and practice them, our prayers can take on new meaning and effectiveness.**

A. Asking

1. **This dimension of prayer communicates need for God's intervention. Even unbelievers at times will pray this kind of desperate plea for help when they have nowhere else to turn. This is often the first experience—beyond memorized prayers—that most people have with prayer.**

Psalm 50:15: "And call upon me in the day of trouble; I will deliver you, and you will honor me."

2. We exercise this prayer anytime we are in need. We seek God and call out to Him during specific troubles.
   a. We are upset and/or harassed.
   b. We are facing dilemmas or we need divine direction for a specific life decision.
   c. We have a strong need or are in trouble.
3. Arrow prayers are usually short and to the point—sent up in a time of need. These prayers lack the praise and repentance aspects spoken of in Session Four.
4. Going to Him when we're in need reminds us of our weakness and keeps us dependent upon Him—it keeps us from getting arrogant and ignoring God.

DISCUSS

Have students suggest one or two examples for each situation mentioned above.

B. Seeking
1. This dimension of prayer communicates a need for intimacy and fellowship with God.

   Read Psalm 23, the shepherd's psalm. Explain: **David spent many hours alone with God, learning about Him and allowing Him to plant His precepts deep in David's heart. Those years on the hillside getting to know and rely on God proved to be David's strength and salvation in the years to come.**
   a. Isaiah 55:6: "Seek the Lord while he may be found; call on him while he is near."
   b. Jeremiah 33:3: "Call to me and I will answer you and tell you great and unsearchable things you do not know."
2. This level of prayer is conversational. Speaking with God on this level should be part of our daily devotions.
   a. Communicate with Him and enjoy a time of intimacy and fellowship.
   b. Pray without desperate need.
   c. Become better acquainted with the Lord, His ways, His expectations and His Word.

REMEMBER

Remember, just because God is ever present and ready to help us does not mean that He is a genie or a butler to us. We should never treat God in an offhand way. Nor should we treat Him as a casual buddy. Even our conversational times with Him should recognize and honor His holiness and sovereignty.

DISCUSS

Have students form small groups and discuss the following:

Why is it important to have times of simple communion with God?

Is this type of prayer effortless? Why do we still have to engage our minds and hearts?

When was the last time you spent a lengthy time with God that wasn't crisis driven? What was the result?

SUGGESTION

Proverbs is an excellent book to read during personal devotions. The sayings are sometimes surprising and life changing! Try memorizing at least one verse each day.

3. Why seek after and call upon God?
   a. We seek God when we have grown cold in our relationship with God and when we know we need to make things right.
   b. Seeking after Him acknowledges His omnipotence.

C. Knocking
   1. "Lord, *help*!" This dimension of prayer communicates deep need—bringing before Him the deep needs of your own soul and the needs of others.

   Psalm 130:1,2: "Out of the depths I cry to you, O LORD; O LORD, hear my voice. Let your ears be attentive to my cry for mercy."

   This is the deepest dimension of prayer. This is where our prayers are full of desperation and heaviness. True repentance, intercession and pleading before God require crying out to Him. God's ear is especially tuned to this type of prayer, because it often requires a greater sacrifice from us.
   2. There are at least four examples of this type of prayer.
      a. Deuteronomy 26:7: The Israelites, crying out from captivity, had this desperation.
      b. 1 Samuel 1:10-16: Hannah cried to God for a son. Words failed her and she approached God at this level.
      c. Luke 8:43-48: The woman who had suffered for eight years with a severe health problem, and who pushed her way through the crowd just to touch the hem of Christ's robe, had this desperation.
      d. Luke 22:39-44: Just before his arrest, Jesus prayed in anguish at this level.
   3. The Lord commanded us to love Him with all of our heart, soul and strength. The deeper the dimension of prayer, the more we understand the fulfillment of this command.

a. Romans 8:26: Understanding that during the times when we are in so much pain that we can't articulate what's in our hearts, the Holy Spirit will make intercession for us

b. Ephesians 6:18: Praying in the power of the Spirit

c. Colossians 4:12: Wrestling in prayer

d. Hebrews 5:7: Praying with loud cries and tears

4. "Praying In the Spirit"

Read Romans 8:26,27: "In the same way, the Spirit helps us in our weakness. We do not know what we ought to pray for, but the Spirit himself intercedes for us with groans that words cannot express. And he who searches our hearts knows the mind of the Spirit, because the Spirit intercedes for the saints in accordance with God's will."

Usually we come to the Lord with our own lists of needs and requests. When we pray in the Spirit, we make ourselves available to pray for what God desires us to pray for. We die to self, and our hearts and minds are aligned with the Spirit's intentions. We can actually feel the impression of the Holy Spirit upon us, guiding our thoughts and prayer. Sometimes we feel a specific direction to pray toward; sometimes we are just urged to pray.

5. "Praying Through"

Read Daniel 10:10-13; then explain: When Daniel prayed and the answer was delayed, he kept on praying. God had sent the answer, but there was conflict in the heavens and the delivery date was postponed.

Sometimes we have to persevere through spiritual battles, sin, lack of faith and even our own emotions before we see the fulfillment of our prayers.

6. Persistence in Prayer

Read Luke 18:1-8; then explain: In this parable, a widow received her answer by going repeatedly to the judge. By the same token, God is even more eager to answer our prayers, but He is teaching us here that often long-term (maybe even over a period of years) persistence in prayer is required of us. The purpose of persistent praying is sometimes a testing of our spiritual determination and faith.

7. Intercessory Prayer

Sometimes we cry out to the Lord on our own behalf. Other times, we are interceding on behalf of someone else. True intercession is when the Spirit of God places in your heart a burden or an intense desire to pray for someone else, or when we see a need ourselves. We become an instrument of blessing from God to others. Praying in the Spirit becomes involved here.

2 Samuel 24:24: "I will not sacrifice to the Lord my God burnt offerings that cost me nothing."

Why do you think this type of prayer accomplishes greater things in the Spirit?	***DISCUSS***

Can you name at least one time in your life when you felt that you had to hear from God, and you prayed until you received an answer? Was it the answer you expected?

How have the times when you truly lost yourself in prayer changed your relationship with God?

• Have students write the names of two people or situations that they will commit to intercessory prayer over the next six months—situations that will require the sacrifice of time, energy and physical comfort so that they can carry them to God consistently and with great intensity.

Reflection

Explain: **Jesus generously repeated in His Word that if we will ask, seek, knock, call, cry and intercede unto Him, He will answer us. He will meet with us daily, in quiet devotions, in times of trouble and when we pour out our hearts like water before Him. Make prayer not a duty but a passionate lifestyle!**

It's not about having a religion—it's about having a relationship!

Take Time

Explain: **Take a quiet walk alone and have a conversation with God. Ask Him for help in learning how to pray in the Spirit and how to practice intercession.**

Closing

Close in prayer.

Lord, Teach Us How to Really Pray

The greatest value in trouble comes to those who bow lowest before the throne.—E.M. Bounds

Goals of This Session

- To help us understand the three different levels of prayer, the differences among them and how each is important to our spiritual walk;
- To explore the deeper, more intense times of prayer: "praying in the Spirit," "praying through" and intercession.

Key Verses

"Arise, cry out in the night, as the watches of the night begin; pour out your heart like water in the presence of the Lord. Lift up your hands to him for the lives of your children, who faint from hunger at the head of every street." Lamentations 2:19

"Ask and it will be given to you; seek and you will find; knock and the door will be opened to you. For everyone who asks receives; he who seeks finds; and to him who knocks, the door will be opened." Matthew 7:7

Biblical Basis

Deuteronomy 26:7; 1 Samuel 1:10-16; 2 Samuel 24:24; Psalms 23; 50:15; 130:1,2; Isaiah 55:6; Jeremiah 33:3; Lamentations 2:19; Daniel 10:10-13; Matthew 7:7; Luke 8:43-48; 18:1-8; 22:39-44; Romans 8:26,27; Ephesians 6:18; Colossians 4:12; Hebrews 5:7

Introduction

God loves to communicate. In turn, He has designed it so that our health, hope and salvation lie in our determination to call upon Him. There is no other way! We simply can't live the Christian life without an active prayer life.

Heartbeat

I. Three Dimensions of Prayer

God's most passionate desire is that we call upon Him. When Jesus instructed us to ask, seek and knock, He wasn't only repeating the same instruction three times. He was teaching us about *three specific levels* of prayer.

A. Asking

1. This dimension of prayer communicates

   _____.

   Psalm 50:15

2. We exercise this prayer anytime we are in need. We seek God and call out to Him during specific troubles.

   a. We are _____.

   b. We are _____ .

   c. We have _____.

3. Arrow prayers are _____

   _____.

4. Going to Him when we're in need reminds us of our _____ and keeps us _____ upon Him—it keeps us from getting _____ and _____ God.

B. Seeking

1. This dimension of prayer communicates a need for intimacy and fellowship with God.

   a. Psalm 23, the shepherd's psalm

b. Isaiah 55:6

c. Jeremiah 33:3

2. **This level of prayer is conversational.**

    a.

    b.

    c.

REMEMBER

Remember, just because God is ever present and ready to help us does not mean that He is a genie or a butler to us. We should never treat God in an offhand way. Nor should we treat Him as a casual buddy. Even our conversational times with Him should recognize and honor His holiness and sovereignty.

SUGGESTION

Proverbs is an excellent book to read during personal devotions. The sayings are sometimes surprising and life changing! Try memorizing at least one verse each day.

3. **Why seek after and call upon God?**

a.   We seek God when _____.

b.   Seeking after Him _____.

C. Knocking

1. "Lord, *help*!" This dimension of prayer communicates _____
    _____.

    Psalm 130:1,2

2. There are at least four examples of this type of prayer.

    a. Deuteronomy 26:7

    b. 1 Samuel 1:10-16

    c. Luke 8:43-48

    d. Luke 22:39-44

3. The Lord commanded us to love Him with all of our heart, soul and
    strength. The deeper the dimension of prayer, the more we understand
    the fulfillment of this command.

    a. Romans 8:26

    b. Ephesians 6:18

    c. Colossians 4:12

    d. Hebrews 5:7

4. **"Praying in the Spirit"**
    Romans 8:26,27

5. **"Praying Through"**
    Daniel 10:10-13

6. **Persistence in Prayer**
    Luke 18:1-8

7. **Intercessory Prayer**
    2 Samuel 24:24

Reflection

Jesus generously repeated in His Word that if we will ask, seek, knock, call, cry and intercede unto Him, He will answer us. He will meet with us daily, in quiet devotions, in times of trouble and when we pour out our hearts like water before Him. Make prayer not a duty but a passionate lifestyle!

It's not about having a religion—it's about having a relationship!

Take Time

Take a quiet walk alone and have a conversation with God. Ask Him for help in learning how to pray in the Spirit and how to practice intercession.

Meditate on the following verses this week:

- Matthew 6:5-13
- Romans 8:26
- Ephesians 6:18
- 1 Thessalonians 5:16-18

Portrait of Prayer

ARE YOU READY TO RUMBLE?!

(GENESIS 32:22-32)

Hang on Jacob! Don't let go! You can do it!

Through the night by the muddy waters of Jabbok, Jacob wrestled with God. Exhausted, he fought until daybreak. Even when his hip was knocked out of joint, he continued the skirmish. This man had determination!

When commanded to release his grip, Jacob said, "Not until You bless me." The bell rang and Jacob's arm was lifted in victory, for he had prevailed. The declaration went forth, "You will no longer be called Jacob, but Israel, because you have struggled with God and men and have overcome."

There are times when our prayers will be a struggle, a battle, a conflict. Despite the hurt, we must pray on and pray through. God responds to our desperation. He admires it! There is blessedness to perseverance. We may walk away limping, but we walk away with the blessing of God resting on our lives.

1. Has there been a time in your life when you have wrestled with God in determination until He has answered? What happened?

2. In which circumstances in your life have you given up too quickly in seeking God?

3. Was God pleased with Jacob?

Shoulder to Shoulder!

Nothing distinguishes the children of God so clearly and strongly as prayer.—E.M. Bounds

Goals of This Session

- To show three areas of the mature Christian life that are critical when it comes to prayer;
- To illustrate how praying together—as husbands and wives, as parents and grandparents, as singles, as single parents and as a church—has a direct affect on the next generation and the destiny of the Church and the nation;
- To motivate us to focus in prayer on these three areas of our lives.

Key Verse

"For where two or three come together in my name, there am I with them."
Matthew 18:20

Biblical Basis

Deuteronomy 4:9; 11:18-21; Ecclesiastes 4:12; Zechariah 4:6; Matthew 18:20; 21:13; Acts 4:1-31; 12:1-18; 16:16-40; Philippians 2:2

Materials and Preparation

- Make copies of this session's student handouts (pp. 210-218).
- Have a white board and dry-erase markers, extra Bibles and pens or pencils available.
- Purchase a ball of ordinary white household twine. It should be made up of about five strands. Cut three two-foot-long pieces of twine. Unravel the first piece into five separate strands. Keep the five strands apart. Unravel the second piece into five separate strands, but keep the five strands loosely together. Keep the intact piece of string separate from the other strands.

Introduction

- Distribute the session handouts.
- Ask a volunteer to read the following information from the introduction of this session's student handouts:

As individuals, prayer is critical to our walk with God. It is the cornerstone upon which everything else in our spiritual lives is built. However, in our family and community relationships, we sometimes fail to implement corporate prayer, which is key to the success of our families, churches and nation. There are three groups discussed in this session: marriage, parents and the Church.

Ask a volunteer to come and break one of the single strands of string. Next ask him or her to break all five loosely held strands. This should be fairly easy to do. Next, ask the volunteer to try to break the piece of string that is in its original shape, all five strands interwoven. This should prove difficult or impossible, even for a strong man.

Explain: **Whether you're married or single, understand that the binding together of two or three persons, pointed out by Jesus in our Key Verse (as well as in Ecclesiastes 4:12), was designed for a specific spiritual purpose. The prayers of two or more people accelerate the energy of the Holy Spirit to a dimension of greater activity. In other words, Jesus was saying that He will accomplish more, faster and with more intensity and power when we bind ourselves together in prayer. Unity strengthens, motivates, inspires, reassures and invigorates! Corporate prayer has the power to bring the Body of Christ together like nothing else can. It is also one of the few practices that transcends denominational differences.**

OBJECT LESSON

Heartbeat

I. Prayer Within Relationships

Philippians 2:2: "Then make my joy complete by being like-minded, having the same love, being one in spirit and purpose."

Have students give examples of what they consider to be important ingredients in a marriage. Some examples might be: communication, trust, compatibility, maturity, mutual attraction, similar interests, patience, etc.

DISCUSS

Explain: There are literally hundreds of ingredients to a successful home—whether you're married and raising a family or are single. However, the most important thing you can do on a daily basis is to pray with others. It's amazing how many Christian couples do not do this regularly. The number of adult singles who lack prayer partners is equally incredible. But the joint spiritual power of two or more people committed to praying together is a formidable force!

A. What Praying Together Does

1. It breaks down barriers caused by life's little irritations and large conflicts.
2. It generates compassion and humility among believers as they pray for one another.
3. It gives peace, strength and comfort to single-parent families.
4. It unites couples and families in a common purpose.
   a. Common dreams and goals
   b. God's help for problems and heartaches
5. It helps remove the feelings of loneliness and helplessness that anyone—married or single—may have when trying to face problems alone.
6. It allows the Holy Spirit to work in knitting the hearts of husband and wife together.
   The spiritual union of a couple completes the cycle of "the two shall become one." Physical and emotional unity is only part of the marriage; it is God's design that spiritual harmony take place as well, and praying together is central to that process.
7. It generates spiritual activity in the home.
   As the fragrance of prayer fills the home, the Holy Spirit begins to work in the hearts of those living there.
8. It brings awareness of areas of need (i.e., for forgiveness between two friends, for more selflessness on the part of children in the home, for more time and attention to be paid to the marriage, etc.).
9. It prepares individuals spiritually for the times when life's storms hit hard and spiritual strength and unity are badly needed.

B. What to Pray for as a Couple

1. Pray for the specific needs of your mate.
2. Pray for God's blessing and protection on your mate.
3. Pray for your mutual goals and dreams.
4. Pray for your mutual difficulties and concerns.
5. Pray for your children.
6. Pray for your extended family, friends, neighbors and coworkers.
7. Pray for the needs and concerns of the Church, community, the nation and the world.

C. What Singles Should Pray For

1. Pray for the specific needs of your close friends and family.
2. Pray for God's blessing and protection on your life.
3. Pray for your goals, dreams and God's will for your life.

4. Pray for your fears, difficulties and concerns.
5. Pray for your children (if you're a single parent).
6. Pray for your extended family, friends, neighbors and coworkers.
7. Pray for the needs and concerns of the Church, community, the nation and the world.

> *Note*: These lists encompass many life issues. The important thing is to pray with another person regularly. For couples, it should be every day. It's never too late to begin building this strong foundation!

II. Parents

A. Passing On a Spiritual Legacy

Deuteronomy 11:18-21: "Fix these words of mine in your hearts and minds; tie them as symbols on your hands and bind them on your foreheads. Teach them to your children, talking about them when you sit at home and when you walk along the road, when you lie down and when you get up. Write them on the doorframes of your houses and on your gates, so that your days and the days of your children may be many in the land that the LORD swore to give your forefathers, as many as the days that the heavens are above the earth."

What are some things that we can pass on to our children? Include habits, weaknesses, talents, personality traits, etc.

BRIEFLY DISCUSS

Whatever else we may pass on to our children, our spiritual legacy is the most important. The daily presence of prayer in the home, coupled with the practice and teaching of godly principles and the Word, is true preparation for adulthood. If your children know how to call upon God, there is always hope in their future.

Do your children ever hear you pray? Are they familiar with the sound of prayer in your home? We need to acknowledge and practice the presence of God in our homes. Make Christ visible! Our children must do three things.

1. They must see us pray.

   They need to know that prayer can take place anywhere and anytime and not just in a kneeling position or with eyes closed!

2. They must hear us pray.

   We must give them blessings, intercede for them and others, give thanks and praise, cover them with protection, etc.

3. They must participate in prayer.

B. What to Pray for Your Children

1. Pray for divine help and wisdom for you, the parent.
2. Pray for God's protection upon your children.
3. Pray that they will keep good friends and company.

4. Pray that they will resist evil influences.
5. Pray that they will hunger after the things of God.
6. Pray for their personal holiness in specific areas.
   a. Their thought lives
   b. Sexual purity
   c. Absence of rebellion
7. Pray for power in the Spirit in specific areas.
   a. To overcome fears and doubt
   b. To trust in God
   c. To become the people God designed them to be
8. Pray for their education and career choices.
9. Pray for their future mates.

C. When to Pray with Your Children
1. Pray in the morning before school.
2. Pray at mealtimes.
3. Pray in times of crisis and need.
4. Pray in times of thankfulness, acknowledging answered prayers.
5. Pray at night before bedtime.
6. Pray together in church.

D. The Grandparents' Role
Grandparents play an increasingly active role in the lives of many children in today's society. Be a prayer partner with your grandchildren. Teach them the ways of the Lord and strengthen the generational bonds in a powerful, spiritual way!

Deuteronomy 4:9: "Only be careful, and watch yourselves closely so that you do not forget the things your eyes have seen or let them slip from your heart as long as you live. Teach them to your children and to their children after them."

I learned more about Christianity from my mother than from all the theologians of England.—John Wesley

III. The Praying Church

A. Becoming a House of Prayer
1. Matthew 21:13: "'It is written,' he said to them, 'My house will be called a house of prayer.'"
2. "If praying is that important . . ."
   "What does it say about our churches today that God birthed the church in a prayer meeting, and prayer meetings today are almost extinct? . . . Americans designate one day a year as a National Day of Prayer. Do we have any right to ask mayors and senators to show up for a special event, with the television cameras rolling, if we don't have regular prayer meetings in our churches? If praying is that important, why don't we do it every week?"[1]—Jim Cymbala

Churches today are so outwardly motivated by trends and paradigm shifts around them, there is a movement away from the simple, foundational truths that defined and energized the Early Church. Unfortunately, although the most important element in the Body of Christ, prayer has often been jettisoned for more user-friendly programs. But make no mistake: Prayer is still number one on God's list of priorities for His Church. Whether large or small, every church has to make many decisions about which program to implement. But there is one thing we *know* that God wants us to do, and that is pray.

Zechariah 4:6: "Not by might nor by power, but by my Spirit, says the LORD Almighty."

The purpose of the Church is to bring people to the throne of grace for mercy and redemption, hope and healing. How do we do that without prayer? Each church must ask itself:

a. Do we have weekly prayer meetings in our church, even if only two or three members show up?

b. How much time is spent in actual prayer during the Sunday service?

c. Are we more concerned with numbers than with whether those of us who are there are actively seeking God and engaging in dynamic prayer?

d. How many of us are familiar with the history of the Church, its revivals and martyrs? How many of us know the sacrifices being made around the world today by the persecuted Church?

Do you want to know your Church's legacy? Read the book of Acts. It is a dramatic tale of the Early Church bursting on the scene and causing havoc of such catastrophic proportions that the Roman government was stood on its head trying to put out the fire of the Holy Spirit. Roman leaders were constantly struggling to round up and eliminate the perpetrators, hoping to vanquish the gospel. Unfortunately for them, they were up against a praying Church. No contest! Nothing can stop the power of desperate people who bind themselves together in prayer. The following are three examples of the power of prayer that our forefathers passed down to us.

B. Miracles and Boldness

Read Acts 4:1-31, the account of Peter and John being brought before the Sanhedrin. Explain: **The two disciples frustrated the priests, the Temple guard and the Sadducees so badly that they were released with a warning. Peter and John went back to their friends and loved ones, told them what happened and had a prayer meeting, calling on God for more boldness, miracles and deliverance. They knew divine help was the only way they were going to get through the days ahead. As they prayed, the whole place was shaken!**

DISCUSS

Have students discuss in small groups:

What specific needs of Peter, John and the Church were met during that prayer meeting?

How would we respond to similar persecution?

What kinds of threats to our religious liberties are we facing today, and how should we pray in response?

C. Breakout!

Read Acts 12:1-18 and explain: **This is the story of Peter's miraculous escape from prison. Peter's release was set in motion by the Church earnestly praying for him.**

DISCUSS

Describe one of your desperate prayers that received an unexpected answer or an answer that came sooner than expected.

D. Whole Lotta Shakin' Goin' On

Read Acts 16:16-40 and explain: **This is the account of Paul and Silas's imprisonment and the earthquake that ensued during their midnight prayer meeting.**

DISCUSS

Have students discuss in small groups:

What do you think it took for Paul and Silas to reach a place in their relationship with God where they were able to pray and sing through their pain, fear and desperation?

If the times we live in are as sinful as we say they are, what are we doing about it? Are we ready for the difficulties or battles that could come our way? As a church, how can we do less than give ourselves fervently to prayer, fasting and the Word? Prayer is our lifeline to God. Everything else should be secondary.

Reflection

Explain: **In our daily lives, we often lose sight of the big picture. But it's good to regularly hold our lives up to the light of history, eternity and present-day reality. The truth is, as Christians we stand in a long line of keepers of the flame, many of whom shed their blood to keep it burning. By standing together in one accord and with the guidance of the Holy Spirit, we can pass on this treasured legacy of salvation to the next generation.**

There Is Strength in Unity!

Take Time

Explain: Discover the power of collaborative prayer! If you're married, cultivate your marriage and family together. If you're single, get involved in a church cell group or Bible study, and worship and pray like you mean it. Pray with passion! Pass it on. As you read, notice the impact that prayer had on the development of the Church.

Pray with the Word. Read the Bible together, perhaps taking turns reading a favorite passage. Memorize verses together. Jot down Scriptures of encouragement for your mate to carry in his or her wallet. God's Word is life and nourishment to every believer, providing peace and solutions in the rough times.

Closing

Close in prayer.

Note
1. Jim Cymbala with Dean Merrill, *Fresh Wind, Fresh Fire* (Grand Rapids, MI: Zondervan Publishing House, 1997), n.p.

Shoulder-to-Shoulder!

Nothing distinguishes the children of God so clearly and strongly as prayer.—E.M. Bounds

Goals of this Session

- To show three areas of the mature Christian life that are critical when it comes to prayer;
- To illustrate how praying together—as husbands and wives, as parents and grandparents, as singles, as single parents and as a church—has a direct affect upon the next generation and the destiny of the Church and the nation;
- To motivate us to focus in prayer on these three areas of our lives.

Key Verse

"For where two or three come together in my name, there am I with them." Matthew 18:20

Biblical Basis

Deuteronomy 4:9; 11:18-21; Ecclesiastes 4:12; Zechariah 4:6; Matthew 18:20; 21:13; Acts 4:1-31; 12:1-18; 16:16-40; Philippians 2:2

Introduction

As individuals, prayer is critical to our walk with God. It is the cornerstone upon which everything else in our lives is built. However, in our family and community relationships, we sometimes fail to implement corporate prayer, which is key to the success of our families, churches and nation. There are three groups outlined in this chapter: marriage, parents, and the Church.

Heartbeat

I. Prayer Within Relationships
Philippians 2:2

A. What Praying Together Does

1. It breaks down _____ caused by life's little irritations and large conflicts.

2. It generates _____ and humility among believers as they pray for one another.

3. It gives _____, strength and comfort to single-parent families.

4. It unites couples and families in a common purpose.
    a. Common_____ and goals
    b. God's help for_____ and _____

5. It helps remove the feelings of _____ and _____ that anyone—married or single—may have when trying to face problems alone.

6. It allows the Holy Spirit to work in knitting the _____ of husband and wife together.

7. It generates _____ activity in the home.

8. It brings _____ of areas of need (i.e., for forgiveness, for more selflessness and generosity, for more time and attention to be paid to the marriage, etc.).

9. It prepares the couple spiritually for the times when life's storms hit hard and spiritual _____ and unity are badly needed.

B. What to Pray for as a Couple

1.

2.

3.

4.

5.

6.

7.

C. What Singles Should Pray For
   1.

   2.

   3.

   4.

   5.

6.

7.

II. Parents

A. Passing On a Spiritual Legacy
Deuteronomy 11:18-21

Whatever else we may pass on to our children, our spiritual legacy is the most important. Do your children ever hear you pray? To understand the importance and the place of prayer in our lives, our children must do three things.

1. They must _____ us pray.
2. They must _____ us pray.
3. They must _____ in prayer.

B. Pray for Your Children
1. Pray for divine help and wisdom for you, the parent.

2. Pray for God's protection upon your children.

3. Pray that they will keep good friends and company.

4. Pray that they will resist evil influences.

5. Pray that they will hunger after the things of God.

6. Pray for their personal holiness in specific areas.

   a.

   b.

   c.

7. Pray for power in the Spirit in specific areas.

   a.

   b.

   c.

8. Pray for their _____ and career choices.
9. Pray for their future _____.

C. Pray with Your Children

   1.

   2.

3.

4.

5.

6.

D. The Grandparents' Role

Grandparents play an increasingly active role in the lives of many children in today's society. Christian grandparents can be of enormous value, through prayer, to the future of their grandchildren. Be a prayer partner with your grandchildren. Teach them the ways of the Lord and strengthen the generational bonds in a powerful, spiritual way!

Deuteronomy 4:9

"I learned more about Christianity from my mother than from all the theologians of England."—John Wesley

III. The Praying Church

A. Becoming a House of Prayer

Matthew 21:13

Zechariah 4:6

The purpose of the Church is to bring people to the throne of grace for mercy and redemption, hope and healing. How do we do that without prayer? There are a few questions each church must ask itself.

1. Do we have weekly prayer meetings in our church, even if only two or three members show up?
2. How much time is spent in actual prayer during the Sunday service?
3. Are we more concerned with numbers than with whether those of us who are there are actively seeking God and engaging in dynamic prayer?
4. How many of us are familiar with the history of the Church, its revivals and martyrs? How many of us know the sacrifices being made around the world today by the persecuted Church?

Want to know the Church's legacy? Read the book of Acts. In it are three examples of the power of prayer that our forefathers passed down to us.

B. Miracles and Boldness

Acts 4:1-31

DISCUSS

Discuss the following questions:

- What specific needs of Peter, John and the church were met during that prayer meeting?

- How would we respond to similar persecution?

- What kinds of threats to our religious liberties are we facing today, and how should we pray in response?

C. Breakout!

Acts 12:1-18

Describe a desperate prayer that received an unexpected answer or an answer that came sooner than expected.

D. Whole Lotta Shakin' Goin' On

Acts 16:16-40

What do you think it took for Paul and Silas to reach a place in their relationship with God where they were able to pray and sing through their pain, fear and desperation?

Reflection

In our daily lives, we often lose sight of the big picture. But it's good to regularly hold our lives up to the light of history, eternity and present-day reality. The truth is, as Christians we stand in a long line of keepers of the flame, many of whom shed their blood to keep it burning. By standing together in one accord and with the guidance of the Holy Spirit, we can pass on this treasured legacy of salvation to the next generation.

There Is Strength in Unity!

Take Time

Discover the power of collaborative prayer! If you're married, cultivate your marriage and family together. If you're single, get involved in a church cell group or Bible study, and worship and pray like you mean it. Pray with passion! Pass it on. As you read, notice the impact that prayer had on the development of the Church.

Pray with the Word. Read the Bible together, perhaps taking turns reading a favorite passage. Memorize verses together. Jot down Scriptures of encouragement for your mate to carry in his or her wallet. God's Word is life and nourishment to every believer, providing peace and solutions in the rough times.

Portrait of Prayer

Daily Appointment
(Daniel)

"Daniel, wake up, son. It's time for your morning prayer." Since as early as he could remember, this was the way his morning would begin. His dad and he would recite together psalms, prayers and Scriptures. Often his sleepy mind and eyes made it look like what his father was implanting in his heart was missing its mark. "Hear, O Israel: The LORD our God, the LORD is one. Love the LORD your God with all your heart and with all your soul and with all your strength" (Deuteronomy 6:4). As faithful as the sun's dawning, so was his father's voice raising him from a deep slumber into prayer each day.

Now sixteen years old, Daniel had developed into a perceptive, sharp, devoted young man. His proud parents envisioned a wonderful future for him.

On this morning, his father's urgent voice awakened him. "Son, the enemy has invaded our country. Quickly dress and come down to pray."

Before the evening light dimmed into a chaotic dusk, Daniel was whisked away by vulgar, brutish soldiers. Ripped from the arms of his family, he was taken prisoner and led away.

Waking up on the hard ground with his face on his rolled-up cloak, reality punched the wind out of his spirit. *Daniel, what are you going to do now that Mom and Dad aren't here to watch over and protect you? You're in a foreign country. Strange people, strange ways surround you. Who is going to be there for you now?*

Blinking back tears of fear, Daniel's lips softly began the cadence, "Hear, O Israel: The LORD our God, the LORD is one."

Three times a day he would go before God, lifting his heart in prayer and intercession. They could tear him away from his family and his homeland, but they couldn't extinguish the flame of hope and faith burning in his heart, ignited by his parents' devotion.

When things went well, Daniel prayed three times a day. When his world would flip upside down, he would also pray. His parents had instilled a devotion to God so deep in his heart that neither exile in a hostile country nor the threat of being dropped into a den of famished lions could persuade Daniel to ignore his daily appointments with his creator, whom he loved with all his heart, all his soul and all his strength.

1. Is my prayer life more consistent in times of prosperity and calm or in times of need and struggle?

2. What level of commitment to God does my prayer life demonstrate?

3. How can I build discipline in my prayer life while maintaining vitality and excitement?

Colorful Ways to Teach Kids About Jesus

God Answers Prayers
Shirley Dobson
Coloring Book
ISBN 08307.27507

God Loves You!
Shirley Dobson
Coloring Book
ISBN 08307.23293

God's Little Helper
Shirley Dobson
Coloring Book
ISBN 08307.21886

God Made the World
Shirley Dobson
Coloring Book
ISBN 08307.24877

Growing as God's Child
Shirley Dobson
Coloring Book
ISBN 08307.26225

Jesus is Alive!
Shirley Dobson
Coloring Book
UPC 607135.000891

Jesus Loves Me!
Shirley Dobson
Coloring Book
ISBN 08307.20715

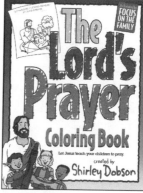

The Lord's Prayer
Shirley Dobson
Coloring Book
SPCN 25116.08987

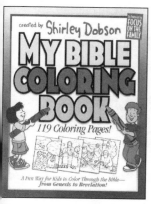

My Bible Coloring Book
Shirley Dobson
Coloring Book
ISBN 08307.20685

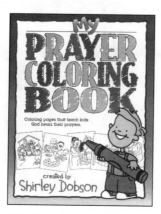

My Prayer Coloring Book
Shirley Dobson
Coloring Book
SPCN 25116.08251

My Family Prayer Calendar
Shirley Dobson
Calendar

Available at your local Christian bookstore • www.gospellight.com

Gospel Light

Gospel Light is God's Word for a Kid's World!

Sunday School Curriculum

What do kids need most today? To know Jesus and have a safe place where they can grow. Gospel Light Sunday School curriculum makes it easy for you to provide that place in your church. From our *Little Blessings Nursery Kit* to *Planet 56* for fifth and sixth grades, Gospel Light provides everything you need: teacher-friendly teacher's guides, colorful and fun student pages, engaging activities, great music and more.

Vacation Bible School

Gospel Light is the creative and fun choice for churches that love to reach children for Jesus. Each summer, we provide a highly evangelistic program that makes it easy for you to create an incredible environment at your church—where children will want to come to experience great Bible stories, skits, crafts, games and songs. It will be the highlight of your children's ministry year!

For every age, and at every time, Gospel Light's flexible programs help you bring God's Word to a kid's world. Try them for yourself and see! For **FREE curriculum samples**, to order a starter kit, or to receive more information, please call your curriculum supplier or **1-800-4-GOSPEL**.

Gospel Light

Pulse

GOD'S WORD
FOR A JR. HIGH WORLD

Young people between the ages of 11 and 14 are the most open to who Jesus is and what a life with Him offers. Reach them with Pulse—designed especially for them!

Throughout the cutting-edge series, 3 categories of study help junior highers understand and apply God's Word in their lives: Biblical, Life Issues, Discipleship.

Connect with junior highers—get all 24 Pulse studies!

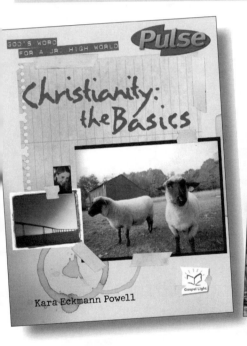

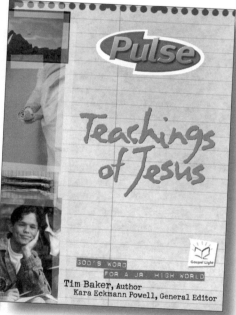

#13 Peer Pressure
ISBN 08307.25490

#14 The Early Church
ISBN 08307.25504

#15 Worship
ISBN 08307.25512

#16 Changes
ISBN 08307.25520

#17 Faith
ISBN 08307.25539

#18 The Great Commission
ISBN 08307.25547

#1 Christianity: the Basics
ISBN 08307.24079

#2 Prayer
ISBN 08307.24087

#3 Friends
ISBN 08307.24192

#4 Teachings of Jesus
ISBN 08307.24095

#5 Followers of Christ
ISBN 08307.24117

#6 Teens of the Bible
ISBN 08307. 24125

#7 Life at School
ISBN 08307.25083

#8 Miracles of Jesus
ISBN 08307.25091

#9 Home and Family
ISBN 08307.25105

#10 Genesis
ISBN 08307.25113

#11 Fruit of the Spirit
ISBN 08307.25474

#12 Feelings & Emotions
ISBN 08307.25482

#19 Love, Sex & Dating
ISBN 08307.25555

#20 What the Bible Is All About
ISBN 08307.25563

#21 Self-Image
ISBN 08307.25571

#22 Spiritual Gifts
ISBN 08307.25598

#23 Hear My Voice
ISBN 08307.25601

#24 Do Unto Others
ISBN 08307.25628

Available at your local Christian bookstore
www.gospellight.com

The National Day of Prayer

A Bit About Us

The National Day of Prayer Task Force is positioned to direct citizens who are searching for help and hope to the One who can meet their personal needs and bring healing to our land. We desire to encourage people in every city and state across our nation to pray throughout the year as a daily spiritual discipline. Prayer *does* make a difference!

Wear Your Passion on Your Sleeve

The *NDP P.R.A.Y. Bracelets* keep the call to prayer close at hand. Fashioned from durable man-made materials with the acronym "P.R.A.Y." woven into them, these one-size-fits-all bands remind us to praise, repent, ask and yield as we come to God. Available in two striking color combinations. (The multicolor symbolizes the redemption story: red for Christ's blood, white for sanctification, green for eternal life, etc.) They include a wallet-sized card that explains the P.R.A.Y. concept.

P.R.A.Y. Bracelet (navy with white lettering)
NPK10

P.R.A.Y. Bracelet (multicolored with black lettering)
NPK12

Keep Your Keys–and Prayers–Close to Heart

Wearing this cool *P.R.A.Y. Lanyard* around your neck will help keep you together! Not only will you feel more organized with this handy and eye-catching accessory, you'll be reminded to come before the Lord in prayer! Each letter stands for a word that will guide you as you pray—praise, repent, ask and yield.

P.R.A.Y. Lanyard
NPK13

Open the Window for a Breath of Fresh Prayer

This eight-minute video conveys the importance of intercessory prayer. The content is a dramatic presentation, which creates a mental image of the "window" of communication God grants us through prayer. It comes with a sermon outline, linking the video to our P.R.A.Y. curriculum. This video will motivate your Sunday school class or small group to seek to learn more about the role of prayer, while setting up the six-week P.R.A.Y. class. Whether in a church, Bible study or family setting, *The Window of Prayer* will inspire viewers to welcome the burden of standing in the gap.

The Window of Prayer Video
NPV09

The Write Way to Express Needs

Journal answers to prayers, jot a prayer request to others or simply use this powerful pen whenever and wherever! The cobalt blue *NDP Professional Pen* comes with the reminder acronym "P.R.A.Y." and the familiar Scripture reference in 2 Chronicles 7:14. Realize the impact in purpose your writing takes when you use this attractive pen!

NDP Professional Pen
NP068

To place an order or find out more about how you can get involved in the National Day of Prayer,

call:

(800) 444-8828

(Mon. - Fri., 6 a.m. - 5:30 p.m. Mountain time)

or write to:

National Day of Prayer Task Force
PO Box 15440
Colorado Springs, CO 80935-5440

The National Day of Prayer Task Force is a project of the National Prayer Committee, Inc. with a 501 © (3) status. We rely on individual donations, foundation support and resource sales. We receive no funds from the federal government or Focus on the Family. If you feel led, we would be thankful to have you as a partner of the National Day of Prayer Task Force.